WE

*Outrageously Committed
to My Marriage*

52 DEVOTIONS

JESUS-CENTERED DEVOTIONS **J.**

JESUS-CENTERED DEVOTIONS
We: *Outrageously Committed to My Marriage*

Copyright © 2017 Group Publishing, Inc.

The story on page 249 is copyright © 2016 Nappaland Communications Inc. All rights reserved. Reprinted by permission. Nappaland.com.

group.com

Credits
Senior Editor: Candace McMahan
Contributing Editors: Stephanie Hillberry, Mikal Keefer, Rick Lawrence, Candace McMahan
Chief Creative Officer: Joani Schultz
Assistant Editor: Lyndsay Gerwing
Art Director: Amy Taylor
Production Artist: Amy Taylor
Cover Art: Amy Taylor
Production Manager: Melissa Towers

To protect the privacy of the individuals who have shared their stories, the names used in this book are pseudonyms, with the exceptions of the names in the stories on pages 129, 241, and 249.

Library of Congress Cataloging-in-Publication Data

Names: Group Publishing.

Title: We : outrageously committed to my marriage.

Description: First American Paperback [edition]. | Loveland, Colorado : Group Publishing, Inc., 2017.

Series: Jesus-centered devotions

Identifiers: LCCN 2017002026 | ISBN 9781470748463 (pbk.)

Subjects: LCSH: Married people--Religious life. | Married people—Prayers and devotions.

Classification: LCC BV4596.M3 W4 2017 | DDC 248.8/44—dc23 LC record available at https://lccn.loc.gov/2017002026

ISBN 978-1-4707-4846-3

10 9 8 7 6 5 4 3 2 1   26 25 24 23 22 21 20 19 18 17

Printed in China.

Table of Contents

Marriage can be…challenging. And it's easy to understand why.

Marriage requires two people, each with unique quirks and differences, to somehow become one.

Even if you marry someone who seems a lot like you, he or she arrives with a set of expectations and values that may be—probably are—different from your own.

Add to *that* challenge the reality that we're not perfect ourselves. We show up at the altar packing some baggage, too.

Plus, life never turns out quite as expected. People get sick. They lose jobs. They clash with in-laws, give in to temptations, and find themselves addicted. And when life gets hard, fixing what's broken can be doubly difficult when navigating the issues with someone else.

Finally, there's this: Our culture urges us to bail out when the going gets tough.

"Don't throw your life away." "He'll never change." "There are other fish in the sea;

why stay with that tuna?" Much of the advice we hear involves cutting our losses.

And there are times that's exactly the right thing to do: Get out. Get away. If you're in a truly abusive situation—emotionally, physically, or sexually—put down this book and get help. Now.

But if your situation is not abusive, consider this: Some people remain outrageously committed to their marriages. They strap in and stand firm in the face of adultery, infertility, bankruptcy, and chronic illness. And in some cases, their marriages not only survive but also thrive.

But how? How is that even possible?

We interviewed a wide range of married Christians, women *and* men, searching for an answer to that question. We've captured their stories here.

We were humbled by their honesty. You will be, too.

All of them, to a person, faced hardships in their marriages that we couldn't see from the outside. Like your marriage, like *every* marriage, there's more to each story than meets the eye.

And we discovered this: Jesus met these people along the way—when their marriages were challenging, when they were joyful, when they were shaken so hard by tragedy that their marriages seemed to be unraveling.

In these 52 stories, you'll catch sight of how Jesus enters into marriages like yours. Sometimes he prompts transformation. Sometimes he ushers in healing. And sometimes he offers consolation in the midst of heartbreak.

But always, always, *always* he brings hope.

So have hope. The Jesus who's outrageously committed to your marriage is also outrageously committed to you.

You're not alone.

I've Been Married Four Times—but Always to the Same Woman

First there was Nancy the bride…

It wasn't only her red-haired, freckled good looks that snagged my attention; Nancy was also smart, interesting, and funny. But those blue eyes certainly didn't hurt.

It took three tries to land a lunch date and another two to take her to dinner, but once we started dating, we never looked back.

Nancy floated down the aisle and into her new role as bride nine months later.

And I couldn't thank God enough that she'd picked me as her husband.

Within a few years, I was married to Nancy the mom…

After two children arrived, that spontaneous, carefree Nancy I had married morphed into a one-woman crisis-management agency.

With day care to navigate, 2:00 a.m. feedings, preschool graduations (who knew that was a real thing?), laundry, dishes, diapers, and a career to keep afloat, lunch dates were few and far between.

As were *any* dates. Or dinners.

I was in an entirely different marriage. Nancy's smile flashed less often—exhausted moms don't have the energy. The easy spirituality we'd shared—Sunday mornings at church, a Christian concert now and then—gave way to plowing through stacks of life stuff.

We prayed together less often…just when we needed to be praying more.

And then there was Nancy the patient…

Within a few weeks of coming down with the flu, Nancy found it difficult to walk. Her speech slurred. She could no longer safely hold our baby.

After a long hospitalization and endless rounds of therapy, she recovered from the autoimmune disease that nearly killed her.

But the woman who shuffled home from the hospital wasn't the woman who had gracefully walked down the aisle a decade before. She was less confident, quieter. She'd felt death brush her shoulder, knew what she had to lose.

Standing by her hospital bed, I'd prayed with a passion I'd never thought possible, but my wife wasn't healed. Not really. Not completely.

Was Jesus teaching us something in her lingering illness? If so, what? And couldn't we have learned the lesson another way?

And now, decades later, I'm married to Nancy the grandmother...

She's everything a grandmother should be: attentive, loving, kind—and once again exhausted. Chasing after toddlers should be an Olympic sport.

But when I see Nancy snuggling little Ambra in her lap, reading Bible storybooks, talking about Jesus, planting seeds, something inside me melts.

This is the woman I married...and I still thank God she saw fit to have me.

I've been married four times—but always to Nancy.

Each time we've slipped into a new life stage, a new Nancy has appeared, and our marriage has reset. It's familiar, but not the same...so I can't be the same either.

I've learned that's what it means to be committed to "we." It's a commitment not just to the woman I met at the altar but also to the woman she becomes.

Because Jesus isn't finished with her yet—or with me.

"And I am certain that **God, who began the good work within you, will continue his work until it is finally finished** on the day when Christ Jesus returns."

—Philippians 1:6, NLT

Think about your own "seasons" of marriage. We all cycle through them. Spring is when you're emerging from a difficult time into something new and fresh. Summer is a time of growth and vibrancy. Fall is a time of harvest, when you experience the "fruit" in marriage. It's also when the growth has stopped and you experience the onset of a "fallow" time in your marriage. Winter is a time of perseverance through struggle. What season are you in right now? What makes you grateful for the season you're in? What is most difficult about it?

Pause and ask Jesus: **"I'm a different person from the one my spouse first married—how have you helped my true identity emerge over the years, and in what ways do you still long for it to emerge?"**

Start doodling or writing here as you wait for an answer or insight. See what happens.

Bargaining With God

I'd been married about five years when I realized that even though I knew the bit about faith being a relationship with Jesus and even though I had a good relationship with him, I was still counting on some fringe benefits for "following the rules."

Case in point: I'd made all the right choices leading into my marriage. I'd prayed about marrying him before he asked and had made certain that I heard a yes from Jesus before accepting. I'd made sure that the man I was marrying was also a Christian. I was a virgin on my wedding day. We went to church. We hosted a small group at our house. We prayed with and for each other.

And then one day I came home to discover a credit card statement I'd never seen before. Apparently my husband had a gambling problem I didn't know about. A few years later, we learned that we couldn't have children. And then after a bout of unemployment, my husband's faith unraveled.

Throughout all of these seasons, I prayed countless prayers. But beneath my proclamations of trust, there was always one little nagging question on my heart:

"But, Lord, I did everything right. Why is this happening to me?"

It's funny how circumstances bring our true beliefs to light. I believed that if I followed Jesus and did the right things, I'd get what I wanted out of life. But absolutely nowhere in the Bible does Jesus promise this. In fact, he promises troubles and suffering. I guess I'd been ignoring all that stuff. It was easy to do until everything went wrong.

Gently, Jesus revealed the flaws in my "I'll do this if you'll do that" faith equation. It's taken a lot of unlearning, and I still need frequent reminders. Through trials and heartache, I've relearned the gospel. Fortunately, it's not called the Good News for nothing. Beneath the struggles, I've learned empathy and patience and experienced the kind of joy you discover only at the end of your rope—the kind that reminds you that the Good News is forever, can't be taken from us, and heals all things, including marriage.

"I have told you all this so that you may **have peace in me**. Here on earth you will have many trials and sorrows. But **take heart, because I have overcome the world.**"

—John 16:33, NLT

We're all tempted to live our relationship with God "transactionally"—meaning we expect to get something from God if we give something. How have you seen this dynamic impact your relationship with God? What has helped you move past a transactional relationship with him and toward a love with no strings attached?

_____

_____

_____

_____

_____

_____

_____

_____

_____

_____

Kicked Out

Brian and I had been married for three weeks when he kicked me out.

Which to me was incredible, since he was so clearly in the wrong.

He had completely ignored my point of view. And then, when I objected, he kicked me out. He said, "It's embarrassing to get a divorce after only three weeks of marriage, but so be it. I'd rather live with the embarrassment than with you."

So I jumped in my car, slammed the door, and went roaring off in the other direction. I drove for half an hour, praying all the while, "Jesus, please show Brian how wrong he is. Please bring him to his knees in repentance."

I drove back to the house and pulled into the driveway, fully expecting Brian to beg me to forgive him.

Instead, he told me to leave. Again.

So again I drove away. And again I asked Jesus to show Brian the error of his ways. I prayed the same prayer again and again.

Calmer now, I returned to the house.

And this time, Brian met me in the driveway and said, "You don't get it, do you? I really meant what I said."

So I left.

I drove and drove. My mind was blank; my heart was numb.

What was I going to do? My pride wouldn't allow me to drive to my parents' house. How could I admit to such an epic failure?

Gradually, as the summer afternoon faded to evening, I began to think about the role I'd played in our fight. I began to put myself in Brian's shoes. I began to understand why he had ignored my point of view and why he had reacted so vehemently.

I began to think that maybe I wasn't entirely right after all.

I asked Jesus to show me my own sin.

And my heart melted.

I drove home, got out of the car, walked up the steps and into the house. Brian was drying the dinner dishes.

Looking him in the eye, I said, "I'm sorry."

And he said, "Me, too."

I learned a valuable lesson that night: I learned to be scrupulously honest with myself, with my husband, and with Jesus.

That lesson has saved our marriage many times in the 25 years we've been married.

Not to mention a lot of gas.

"**Blessed is the one whose sin the Lord does not count against them** and in whose spirit is no deceit."

—Psalm 32:2

Think about the last argument you had with your spouse. Looking back, what's something you needed to own but didn't? Ask yourself: "Typically, how honest am I with my spouse, Jesus, and myself about my role in arguments and tension in my marriage?" What's one thing you can own about yourself today, and how can you communicate it?

Diary of a Marriage

We'd been married about a week when I got a love note from my wife.

She'd tucked it in my brown-bag lunch, so it came with a peanut butter sandwich: "I love you more than peanut butter itself. Even the crunchy kind."

Now *that's* love.

The next day she found a note from me taped to the bathroom mirror: "This face is the one I think of and miss all day."

It wasn't long before we decided the easiest way to leave messages for each other was to write in a little notebook we kept on our dresser. I'd write to her, she'd write to me, and over the last 25 years, we haven't missed more than a few days.

We've had to replace the notebook dozens of times, and those notes tell the story of our marriage.

There's the time she wrote, 114 times, "I love you." Not because she *felt* that way (it was following an argument in which I was, not for the first time, stubborn beyond belief) but because she was determined to keep writing until she felt the truth of what she was writing. It took a while. Sometimes it still does.

And there's my note telling her I didn't like her new haircut, that I preferred the style she'd worn for several years. That comment should have been delivered face to face, and she let me know it.

Notes scribbled in pencil or ink—black, purple, red—the pages are filled with words meant to connect and encourage.

And just a few years ago, Karen added something new: Bible verses. Reminders that we're not alone in this thing, that Jesus walks with us.

That nothing separates us from God's love shared in the person of Jesus.

That those who love humbly will be blessed.

That putting one another first is the Kingdom way to build a marriage.

Were the fire alarm to sound and I had just moments to rescue what I could, Karen would be my first priority. But, if I could, I'd also scoop up those notebooks and carry them with me to safety.

They're a love story. *Our* love story.

A love story we share with Jesus.

"So **encourage each other and build each other up**, just as you are already doing."

—1 Thessalonians 5:11, NLT)

Maybe writing notes to your spouse isn't really your thing. But why not experiment with it today? Write a note and put it in a place where your spouse will be sure to see it. Nothing long, nothing complicated—just a simple reminder of your commitment and love.

Consider what sort of "love note" you could write to Jesus. Use the space here to tell him what's on your heart. After that, ask Jesus, **"What's your love note to me?"** Wait in silence to "hear" his response—it could be a word, a phrase, a Bible passage, or a picture in your mind. Whatever it is, receive it.

A Fairy Tale

Our story begins in childhood. We met in elementary school when my dad became the pastor of David's parents' church. We became friends in middle school, dated throughout high school, fell deeply in love in college, and married as soon as I graduated. Two beautiful kids and 28 years later, here we are.

This might sound like a fairy tale, but even in fairy tales there are dragons to slay. One of our biggest has been the dragon of my depression. Even in my childhood, the dragon would occasionally peek its head out of its cave, and I would do my best to beat it back with the small sticks and pebbles at my disposal. When David and I married, he became one of the weapons in my arsenal by helping me talk it through and just continually being there in the bad times.

That sort of worked until about nine years ago, when the dragon came fully out of its cave and began a scorched-earth offensive.

I sank from one new low to another. I cried for no reason. I snapped at our young children. Every word I uttered was tinged with hopelessness. I met every new idea with skepticism and cynicism. Even a simple question like "What would you like for dinner?" sent me into a free fall.

At this point, David did the hardest, yet kindest, thing possible. He told me that the dragon was no longer just defeating me; it was hurting him, and, more important, it was hurting our kids. He told me that if I didn't seek professional help, he and the kids would go somewhere safe, somewhere away from me.

That got through. My husband has always been absolutely committed to our marriage. I knew that losing him and the kids would destroy me. So I saw a doctor; David and I sought wise, godly counsel; and every morning since, I take a tiny white pill. The dragon is not completely defeated, but it's back in its cave.

Occasionally, I find my medication too bitter a pill to swallow, and I "forget" to take it for a while. After all, I'm doing so well, and I think that as a Christian I should be able to conquer this on my own. My husband is always the first to remind me that I can't and I don't have to try. Together we pick up and sharpen the sword, and one more time we drive the beast back into its cave.

When I think of all that David has endured during my darkest times, I really do see him as my knight in shining armor.

But I realize what I'm actually seeing when I look at him is the reflection of the Ultimate Dragon Slayer. The One who did the hardest but kindest thing imaginable when he defeated the devil dragon himself by laying down his life. All so that we really do get to live happily ever after.

"Husbands, go all out in your love for your wives, exactly as Christ did for the church—**a love marked by giving, not getting**. Christ's love makes the church whole. His words evoke her beauty. **Everything he does and says is designed to bring the best out of her**, dressing her in dazzling white silk, radiant with holiness. And that is how husbands ought to love their wives. They're really doing themselves a favor—since they're already 'one' in marriage."

—Ephesians 5:25-28, MSG

Jesus lays down his life for us, not just on the cross but in every way. What has it meant to "lay down your life" in your marriage? How have you done it? How has your spouse done it for you? Jesus said we are (truly) his body, the way in which he's able to move into the lives of others and impact them for good. How has your spouse acted as the outward expression of Jesus in your life? Write what comes to you here…

Amnesia

Several years ago I quit a job I hated. Right before Christmas I walked into my boss's office and handed him my resignation. When I went home to tell my husband, he was stunned. And then I was stunned that he was stunned.

We'd talked about this decision, and I thought we were on the same page. *Apparently not*. As we came to terms with our flagrant miscommunication, I also had to endure the discomfort of his discomfort with my new situation.

I immediately went to work on a new venture, but for a solid year, we argued nearly every weekend about my choice to leave my job and start working from home. It was during this time that I learned how to cultivate amnesia.

Here's what I mean…

Like most couples, we'd say things we didn't mean when we argued. He'd launch insults, and I'd counter with some of my own. It wasn't pretty. I'd frequently go to sleep crying into my pillow, praying that Jesus would help us get through this tension and heal our hearts.

I began to recognize that Jesus was answering my prayers in an unexpected way. My normal response after an argument was to mentally replay the fight again and again, stewing over what was said and thinking of comebacks. But after I started praying, I began to notice that I was dwelling less and less on the fights. Instead, I'd get into bed and just fall asleep.

I also started noticing that I didn't remember much of what was said during the arguments the night before. It was as if I'd developed a really bad memory. It wasn't hard for me to recognize what a gift and answer to prayer this was.

Giving me the strength to let go of these fights and to forget what was said during them was Jesus' way of protecting my heart—and our marriage—during this rough patch. Since then I've taken the hint and have been intentional about cultivating a bad memory when it comes to fights and insults. I work harder at letting go and forgetting than I do at winning arguments. This has become a key to staying upbeat, hopeful, and positive in our marriage, especially during rocky times. I never would have thought of forgetfulness as a sign of a good marriage, but it's worked well for us.

"Love...keeps no record of being wronged."

—1 Corinthians 13:5, NLT

What are hurtful words or actions that you tend to bring up to your spouse, perhaps again and again? Would you say you and your spouse have a pattern of healthy forgetfulness in your marriage? Is so, how did you cultivate that? If not, what can you do today to move in that direction? Stop first to invite Jesus to help you: "Jesus, make me forgetful in the best possible way."

Changing Expectations

Something came up at work that required me to stay late, and then backed-up traffic added another 20 minutes to my drive home. I pulled into the garage after dark.

"I'm home," I announced. Within seconds, chubby, grubby hands grabbed my knees, and more tugged at my side. "Hi, girls," I said. "Did you miss me?" My daughters smiled, and then the little one lost her balance, fell over, and started crying.

Balancing my bag, a pizza box, and a crying toddler, I sighed. "Where's your dad, anyway?"

Two minutes later he rounded the corner, scooped the toddler out of my arms, and had her laughing in about six seconds. Of course. As the stay-at-home parent, he's always the one who gets her to calm down.

"You got pizza?" he asked.

"Uh…yeah. I was running late and thought it would be nice not to have to cook."

"I could have made us dinner," he said in a disapproving tone.

"I know, but pizza sounded good."

"Whatever you say," he replied, turning his back on me and heading into the other room.

A year earlier, when my husband came home and announced he'd been laid off, I immediately petitioned my boss to increase my hours to full-time. We assumed that it was temporary, but a year later my career was taking off, and my husband had assumed the role of stay-at-home parent by default. We still weren't used to the arrangement.

I couldn't explain why I felt uncomfortable letting him make dinner all the time, clean the house, and take care of the kids. Partly I'd always pictured myself doing the whole "home" thing while my husband worked. Partly I disapproved of his decision not to rejoin the workforce. I was doing really well in my career but felt we should be earning our income together.

The tension between us continued throughout dinner, and after we put the kids to bed, I confronted him about his attitude.

"We've already talked about this," he said. "It screws up my plan when you bring dinner home without giving me a heads-up. I'd already defrosted chicken."

We sat in silence with the TV on, both lost in our own thoughts. Then a line from the sitcom we were watching caught my attention. It was as if the Holy Spirit had turned up the volume.

"I don't know why I've been fighting it," the character said. "She's way better at managing than me. I should just let her do it and focus on what I can bring to this company."

Jesus was speaking to me through this superficial TV conversation. "Why are you fighting him?" he asked me. "He's good with the girls. He's good at managing the budget. The house is cleaner than when you were home."

Jesus was right. My husband *was* good at this. He did it in his own way, and his ways were different from mine, but it was working. Just like it was working for me at work. I actually enjoyed my job, and I was good at it. The whole scenario just didn't match my idea of how things should be, and I was having a hard time letting go of my expectations. But I wondered if holding on to them was blinding me to the good things that were happening now.

I decided right then to follow Jesus' lead. Turning to my husband, I said, "You're right. I shouldn't bring dinner home without checking with you first. I'm sorry. Chicken tomorrow night?"

"Sure," he said. He didn't know it, but we'd just turned the corner.

"I am not saying this because I am in need, for I have learned to be content whatever the circumstances. I know what it is to be in need, and I know what it is to have plenty. I have learned **the secret of being content in any and every situation,** whether **well fed or hungry,** whether **living in plenty or in want. I can do all this through him who gives me strength."**

—Philippians 4:11-13

Our broken expectations in life can "go to seed," sprouting up as resentment and cynicism and frustration. What unmet expectations do you have in your marriage, and how might they have gone to seed? In the parable of the wheat and the weeds (Matthew 13:24-30), Jesus told us that we are to leave the "weeding" to him. Stop for a moment and ask him to weed your marriage, pulling up anything that has been allowed to go to seed.

Expecting Perfection

There should be an eleventh commandment: "Thou shalt not attempt home improvement projects with thy spouse, for upon these rocks hath many a marriage been dashed to shards and splinters."

I say that because, while my marriage to Tracy survived illness, anger, and fractured finances, it nearly went belly up over wallpaper.

Tracy was pregnant with our firstborn when she announced one Saturday morning that *this* was the day we'd hang wallpaper in the nursery. Because, she explained, the right wall covering was part of providing proper visual stimulation to encourage our soon-to-arrive son's artistic development.

I didn't claim to know much about childhood development, but even I knew the kid would be blind as a bat for the first few months. Assuming our new son noticed the walls at all, they'd be nothing but fuzzy blobs floating on the horizon.

So what was the urgency?

Which is *precisely* the wrong question to ask a pregnant woman.

Wallpapering a room is supposed to be a cinch: Take off the old stuff, clean the wall, hang the new stuff. Simple…in theory.

In addition to our complete lack of experience, there was the nursery itself: three doors, three windows, and not one truly 90-degree angle in the place. And the wallpaper Tracy chose was a plaid. About a zillion points where the pattern had to align—exactly.

It went…poorly. Spectacularly poorly. *Astoundingly* poorly. By noon Tracy was in tears, and I was ready to sell the house—as is—and move anywhere that didn't require wallpaper.

Voice rising, I asked, "Why does this matter? If it's off an eighth of an inch, who'll care? Who'll even notice?"

"*I'll* notice," she sobbed. "If we can't even get *this* right, how will we get anything *else* right?"

And there it was, lying on the floor between us: the heart of the matter.

We'd decided this parenting thing was all about *us*. About *our* getting it right. We were shouldering the load, and if we couldn't work through a simple wallpaper fiasco, how could we handle the big stuff of parenting?

Jesus shows up in odd places, and I believe one of them was that half-finished nursery. I say that because on that Saturday morning, Tracy and I finally looked at each other and admitted we were in over our heads. Way over our heads.

We needed Jesus to show up, not just in our marriage but also in the parenting piece of our marriage. We weren't going to get it right, couldn't *possibly* get it right, and together we needed to lean on Jesus for help.

I can't tell you what a freeing moment that was for us. Jesus wasn't expecting perfection from us, just faithfulness.

And he took it from there.

We finished the wallpapering (tip: always wrap up behind a door; that's where mistakes are least noticeable), and our son and then a daughter passed through that nursery. They survived, and so did our marriage.

A marriage that has never, not for one day, been perfect.

"Jesus answered, 'If you want to be perfect, **go, sell your possessions and give to the poor,** and you will have treasure in heaven. **Then come, follow me.'**"

—Matthew 19:21

This passage is usually used to point out the dangers of money. But read it again. It's also Jesus' answer to living a "perfect" life—it means pursuing him more earnestly than we pursue financial success or any other substitute god. It's the only perfection in life that we have a chance of attaining. And following Jesus is possible. You're doing it right now, in your own messy way.

In some way, your marriage is destined to be flawed because, face it, you're in it. But what does following Jesus actually mean? When you've felt most like you're actually following him, what has that season been characterized by? And in what way can you invite your spouse to join you in following him today?

Drifting Apart

"**R**aising kids," the experts warn, "can't be the only thing holding your marriage together. Make sure you have more in common with your spouse than parenting."

Easier said than done, right?

In theory this advice makes sense. In practice, staying connected to your husband year after year is way harder than it seems. I know this from personal experience.

When my husband and I were first married, we'd stay up for hours, talking and dreaming about our future. Maybe it was just young love, but it *seems* we had a lot in common back then.

But somewhere along the way, our conversations became about kids and budgets and the logistics of being married. These demands kept us involved with each other in a way that felt like closeness, which is why I was surprised when the arguing started.

Most of the time these arguments were just garden-variety disputes. But then, slowly—almost too slowly to notice—the arguments shifted, and I noticed my heart getting heavier, bit by bit. For a long time, I ignored the warning signs, but on some level I knew that ordinary frustration was masking deeper emotions like contempt, regret, and resentment. In the midst of busyness, family time, and even laughter, the Holy Spirit was whispering, "Pay attention to this. It's important."

One morning I was sitting in my armchair with a mug of coffee when the words from a recent argument washed over me:

"You don't listen to me anymore."

"It doesn't matter. You don't notice anyway."

"Whatever. There's no point in talking about this. We'll just end up saying the same things we always do."

I realized with sudden and alarming clarity how disconnected my husband and I had become. The two circles of our lives overlapped only as parents. We weren't interested in the same things anymore. We shared our schedules, shopping lists, and worries about our kids, but I couldn't remember the last time we'd really shared our *hearts* with each other.

"It's bad, Lord," I prayed. "Much worse than I thought. I'm scared. What if we can't fix this?"

"Finally, you're listening," Jesus replied. "It's not too late, but it *is* time to start paying attention and to start praying. I'll help you."

I had a long talk with my husband that night. We were both honest—sometimes brutally honest—in a way we hadn't been in a long time. This honesty was a little scary, but I also felt hopeful after getting everything out in the open. Jesus was on our side, and he would help us. We just needed to pay attention.

"I appeal to you, dear brothers and sisters, by the authority of our Lord Jesus Christ, to **live in harmony with each other**. Let there be no divisions in the church. Rather, **be of one mind, united in thought and purpose**."

—1 Corinthians 1:10, NLT

Draw two circles, one representing your interests and activities and the other representing those of your spouse. **Where do the circles overlap? What encourages you about this? What troubles you?** Now stop and ask Jesus for his guidance in bringing up what's troubling you in a respectful, honoring way. Then take a few minutes to jot some ideas here…

In-Laws

Less than a year after we were married, my husband shoved my sister against the side of a car and told her he never wanted to see her again.

And so began the worst period of my life.

In retrospect, I realize the tension between Mike and Beth had been growing for some time. They grated on each other. Her ways of responding to life struck him as manipulative and controlling. He was volatile and hot-tempered, and she viewed him as someone who had to be managed.

Their relationship exploded during a family camping trip.

After the explosion, after everyone had hurriedly packed up and left the campsite—I in someone else's car, Mike in ours—I had a long, three-hour drive to contemplate my future. And when we met at home and I found that Mike was unrepentant, shouting he'd do it all over again if he had the chance, I felt I had no choice but to leave him.

How could I stay married to a man who I couldn't count on to be kind to my family?

Over the next several days, I consulted friends and family members. All of my family felt I should divorce him. And all of my friends—except one—agreed. The friend who felt I should stay said, "Stick with him. He's rough around the edges, but he's worth it."

Two weeks after the horrible events at the campsite, I still didn't know what to do. As I drove to work early one morning, I was sobbing as I prayed, "Jesus, please show me what to do. My heart says to stay, but my head says to go."

In Jesus' unmistakable, inaudible voice, I heard, "Why does your head say to go?"

"Because he has the emotional quotient of a 12-year-old. Because he'll never change. Because I'm not getting any younger, and it's stupid to throw good time after bad."

"And why does your heart say to stay?"

"Because I love him so much."

And Jesus' answer was as clear as if it had been said out loud for the world to hear: "Then I'll give you what you need."

And he did.

For two years, I woke up every morning fueled by anger and the memories of how my husband had hurt my sister. I would get out of bed and go for an hour-long walk in every kind of weather. For the first half of the walk, my mind would rail against my husband as I replayed those campsite images again and again. By the time I reached the halfway point of my walk, I had exhausted my rage and was ready for Jesus to minister to me. By the time I reached home, I could honestly pray, "Jesus, please give me what I need to get through this day and to honor you."

And he did.

The truth is, I didn't know from hour to hour what I would need. It might be patience. It might be forgiveness. It might be grace. It might be the ability to keep my mouth shut. But whatever it was, Jesus gave it to me, again and again and again.

For two years I spent Christmas morning with my husband and his family and Christmas afternoon with my family. Easters were spent the same way.

Every holiday was a piercing reminder of how broken my family was.

And then my husband's mother died. And my sister came to the funeral.

I'll never forget the sight of my valiant, vulnerable sister, walking down a long hallway at the church, headed straight for my husband with no idea of how he would receive her.

She walked right up to him, put her arms around him, and whispered, "I'm so sorry."

And that was the beginning of the rest of my life.

"Let the morning bring me word of your unfailing love, for I have put my trust in you. **Show me the way I should go, for to you I entrust my life.**"

—Psalm 143:8

Think about the struggles you've faced in your marriage. If you've ever gone through a season in which you intentionally relied upon Jesus every day, what was the outcome? Describe that experience here...

Instinct

Winter can be a hard time in my marriage. The short days, the barrenness, the cold—these outside conditions seem to work their way inside as well. My husband and I both struggle more with depressed feelings and darker thoughts during winter months. Hope and affection are harder to come by, too.

My husband tends to disconnect and withdraw during these times. Naturally this freaks me out. So I do what most wives do. I try to draw him into conversation over dinner. I try to gauge his mood in the morning and amp up the cheerfulness if he seems down. I invest more time in him. I offer more affection and sex.

My instinct is to pull near, to help, to connect.

But here's a secret that Jesus has been teaching me lately: My instinct is wrong. The truth is that all this effort (and it is a *lot* of effort) is driven by fear.

I'm a woman, and when my husband disconnects, I'm afraid—down-to-my-bones afraid. I react by becoming the supportive super-wife, as if a frenzy of helpful nurture will protect me from harm.

And then, when I'm emotionally exhausted, lonely, and frustrated with this husband who clearly isn't rallying to my energetic campaign, I resort to prayer. This is what Jesus says to me:

"Retreat. Let go. Connect to me instead."

It's the *exact opposite* of what my instinct tells me to do.

But it works.

So I pull back. I quit trying to be cheerful when he's down. I spend more time doing the things I want to do and less time with him. I stop asking questions to draw him out. I even cut back on my fervent (fearful) prayers for him.

And it's uncomfortable; it feels wrong.

But eventually, in the midst of discomfort, I find freedom. I remember that God is even more invested in my marriage than I am; he wants us to make it, and he's willing and able to help. And eventually, when my husband is ready, he always reaches out again. And I'm willing and waiting when he does, just as God is willing and waiting for us, always.

"You will keep in **perfect peace** those whose minds are steadfast, **because they trust in you."**

—Isaiah 26:3

In what ways, if any, do you live in fear in your marriage? How do you typically attempt to address or overcome that fear? What patterns of fear-response have surfaced in your marriage? Take a minute to ask Jesus to show you a fresh, new approach, and then follow his lead.

Our Fifth Anniversary

We met while working in a church. We were both committed to following Jesus and helping others come to know him. We loved Jesus, and everything in our lives was centered around him. Our marriage began with vows committing us not only to each other but also to Jesus. The foundation of our marriage was the authority of Christ. This was no half-hearted faith. This was the essence of our life together.

On our fifth anniversary, we feasted on delicious food and each other's company, with lots of laughter and uninterrupted conversation. As we reflected on the past year, we waded into deeper conversational waters. We asked each other what we could do differently in the coming year to better love and serve the other. Carefully, tenderly, we ventured into this part of the discussion. Constructive criticism is never easy to give or receive, but we've always believed that, when given in love and received with an open heart, it can do so much good.

I cautiously broached the subject that had been on my mind for a while. I asked if he would start praying with the kids and me more often, if he'd assume a greater role as the spiritual leader of our family.

I was completely blindsided by his response.

He said he'd been wrestling with keeping *any* faith in Christ. He had so many unanswered questions and doubts. For years he'd been struggling to reconcile the big questions and pains in life with the existence of a loving God. Being the intelligent, analytical man he is, he *hoped* but was finding it difficult to *believe* that there was much legitimacy to faith in God.

I was confused. Shocked. Of course people change over time, but this? This was not the marriage I'd agreed to. This was not how I'd planned to raise our children—in a home divided by faith. This changed everything: the intricacies of our marriage relationship, the communities and groups we could be involved in, and even how we structured our everyday living and seasons of celebration. We no longer had a common vision or goals. Everything felt divided and messy and tense. My whole life and all my expectations for our marriage and family seemed to be crumbling.

Over the next couple of years, I experienced huge swings of emotion, feeling hopeful one day and discouraged and angry the next. We went through seasons of denial followed by seasons of intense discussion and wrestling with how to be married well despite the growing tension, division, and disappointment.

I did a lot of arguing, yelling, and crying in a desperate attempt to convince my husband to reclaim his faith, but nothing I did was making a difference—at least not the difference I hoped for. Most of my words were destructive, and looking back I'm sorry I ever spoke them.

I knew I needed to trust God to work in my husband's heart, but I was convinced that God needed my help to poke and prod my husband back toward him. I was grasping for control in every way I knew how.

At first I felt isolated and alone. But as I was struggling to trust God during those difficult years, Jesus was at work (as he always is), surrounding me with people who encouraged me on this difficult journey. I felt embarrassed and unsure of how to move forward, but after a while I knew I would. After all, I had committed to love and honor my husband for better or worse, and it was time to learn how to really do this.

Little by little, the Holy Spirit filled me with the assurance that God sees. He knows. He cares. He desires that all should be saved and that none perish. I began to truly believe that Jesus can accomplish far more than I could ever even begin to ask or imagine and most definitely more than all my anxious words could achieve.

I wish I could finish this story by tying it up with a tidy little bow. But the truth is, we're still in the thick of it. And it's hard—really hard. But now I have peace. Not because I know how our story will end, but because I know God is with me. I don't like this journey, but I know I'm not alone. I know God hasn't forgotten. He's at work. He's up to something—in my heart and in my husband's. In the meantime, I continue to wait, to ask, and to trust.

"The Lord is not slow in keeping his promise, as some understand slowness. **Instead he is patient with you,** not wanting anyone to perish, but everyone to come to repentance."

—2 Peter 3:9

This author has entered a time of waiting, of trusting Jesus without any assurance that the outcome she hopes for will come to pass. In your marriage, how have you learned to wait and trust that Jesus will act? Does this come easily, or is it hard for you, and why? What's something you can, right now, slide over to him as his responsibility, instead of working hard to make it happen? What's something true about Jesus' heart that gives you confidence to trust him with this?

The Miracle
of Our Marriage

I've heard that a shepherd will break the legs
of a lamb that chronically wanders away from the
flock. What a seemingly cruel solution! But once the
shepherd breaks the little lamb's legs, the shepherd is
bound to that lamb for its survival. He must hand-feed
and water the animal. Moreover, the shepherd carries
the lamb over his shoulders until its legs have healed.
It's during this time that the lamb and shepherd forge a
deeply loving and intimate relationship.

And that's really been the story of my marriage.

I vividly remember our wedding day, dancing our first
dance to "Have I Told You Lately That I Love You?" On
that day, I knew I had arrived. This born-in-a-trailer-park

girl had met her prince, and the life ahead of us could be nothing but shiny and beautiful.

During the first few years of our union, we were intent on playing…and playing hard. Wearing the DINK (double income no kids) badge proudly, we honeymooned in the wine country, partied, and traveled in pursuit of the perfect meal and bottle of wine.

Then we decided we were far too fabulous in both our DNA and our untested parenting skills not to have children…and within a month, I was pregnant.

Baby #1 arrived, followed closely by Baby #2. I was addicted to control, so motherhood was not easy, but it was made much worse by bouts of postpartum depression resulting in severe insomnia. My husband suffered deeply as he watched me try to cope.

Then, 18 months into parenting our second child, we found ourselves in a sterile medical office at Children's Hospital. There were six adults and two small children crammed into this extremely small room. I heard, as if from a distance, a jumbled string of words: "Genetic, chronic, double delta DNA strands, lung failure, life-abbreviating…about 32."

In that swirl of sound, I heard only one thing clearly: "Daughter, I am your great High Priest. I have faced the same trials you and your sweet baby have, and I understand." I remembered reading somewhere that the clinical cause of Jesus' death as he hung on the cross was lung failure. He was in his early 30s. I wept.

Ninety percent of marriages fail under the pressure of parenting a chronically ill child. I ran to my control addiction for comfort, and my husband began romancing alcohol. I found myself acting essentially as a single parent and, on a different layer of my soul, feeling murderous toward my husband. Our lives were crumbling around us.

But something odd—something supernatural—was happening. As I asked Jesus to show me how to love my husband as Jesus does, a precious gem was protected in my heart. This gleaming stone, beautiful and unmoving, contained treasured remembrances of how deeply I love my husband. Deep in my heart was a continual declaration: "Gift. Treasure. He is so cool! I am the luckiest girl. No man is better than my man." And on and on.

I remember telling my husband during this time that Jesus was jealous after him and relentlessly pursuing him. My wise (but at that time annoying) husband replied, "Jesus is pursuing *you*." So, in my single-parenting, I desperately and humbly asked Jesus to husband me. And he did. Jesus not only shepherded me but also husbanded me. It seemed that everywhere I went I heard the song "Have I Told You Lately That I Love You?" In the car, on the radio, in malls, in grocery stores, in ice cream shops, in pizza places—it became seriously funny.

I'm thankful that my single-parenting stint didn't last long (it's a really hard job!), but our marriage wasn't healed overnight. My husband's behavior when he was drinking too much had seriously wounded me and obliterated any idea of shiny and beautiful... except for the protected, unmoving gem in my heart. "Gift. Treasure. He is so cool! I am the luckiest girl. No man is better than my man."

Now, many years later, I walk in the miracle of my marriage every day. Statistically, we shouldn't be married. But ours is not the God of statistics. He is the God of impossibilities. The Seeker, Shepherd, and Redeemer of the one lost lamb.

"If a man owns a hundred sheep, and one of them wanders away, will he not leave the ninety-nine on the hills and go to look for the one that wandered off? And if he finds it, truly I tell you, **he is happier about that one sheep than about the ninety-nine that did not wander off."**

—Matthew 18:12-13

The truth is, we all wander off from time to time. Take some time this week to think about the times you've wandered off and the methods Jesus used to bring you back into the fold. What did you learn about Jesus during these times? Write your thoughts here…

Friends

Not all friends are created equal when it comes to helping you through rough times in marriage.

When my marriage started to flounder a few years ago, I reached out to the people close to me. Over coffee dates and texts and dinners, I disclosed the details. After a couple of months, I noticed that certain friends left me feeling encouraged and hopeful. Others left me feeling sad.

I asked Jesus to help me figure out what was going on. He answered by showing me what supportive friendship looks like based on how his close friends cared for one another. A friend isn't shocked by your darkness, whatever it is: infidelity, pornography, selfishness. A friend helps you bring your darkness into the light of Christ. A friend doesn't judge or shame you *or* your spouse. A friend lovingly listens, comforts, and supports you.

A friend can be trusted to maintain your confidence and doesn't gossip about your situation. A friend can also be trusted to extend grace and forgiveness to you and your spouse.

A friend supports your decisions while also cheering for your spouse. A friend hopes for reconciliation and points you back to your spouse by reminding you of the kind of love Jesus extends to us, which is sacrificial and full of grace.

A friend lets you know if your situation is dangerous and if you need to get out. A friend finds ways to get you help and protection.

Jesus showed me that not all of my friends could navigate this hard but precious time in my life and that it was important to find people who could. I began sharing more with the friends who could and pulling back from those who couldn't. And I was on the lookout for new, trustworthy friends to bring into my circle. They all had one thing in common: They shined the light of Jesus into the dark places in my marriage. And with their help, the light consumed the darkness.

"Wise words are like deep waters;
wisdom flows from the wise like a bubbling brook."

—Proverbs 18:4, NLT

Think about the friends who leave you feeling encouraged and hopeful after talking with them about the difficult things you're going through. What do they have in common? Thank Jesus for putting them in your life, and take a minute to pray that other people struggling with hard things will find friends like them, too. Then ask the Holy Spirit to show you how you can be that kind of friend to someone else right now.

Prayer

After all these years I suppose I can finally confess: I spied on my parents. I think all kids must do that from time to time; it's one way we come to understand how to be grown-ups.

But what I caught them doing changed my life— and later my marriage.

When I was a child, I sometimes found myself needing something from my parents after bedtime. A test signed, money for a field trip—it seemed there was always something I'd forgotten to ask about.

So I'd crawl out of bed and pad softly down the hall to their room.

And because they slept with the door ajar so they could hear if one of us kids got scared or sick during the night, I could also hear them. And if I peeked, I could see them as well.

And that's how I first peered through the narrow crack of the slightly open door and saw them side by side, kneeling by their bed and praying.

The first time it was an accident. But before long I often found myself standing outside their door, listening as they prayed for my brother, my sister, and me.

It warmed my heart to know I was loved so much. And I was reassured that no matter what was happening at school or in the world, I wasn't alone. They were with me, and so was Jesus.

I carried their example with me into my marriage. I love nothing more than to lie in bed with my husband, praying as we're wrapped in each other's arms. Sometimes we're laughing as we pray, sometimes we're weeping, but we're always there praying.

It's meeting Jesus in prayer that's kept our world from crumbling during the dark days of losing our infant son; of coping with a grown daughter going to jail; of enduring illnesses, disappointments, and all the aches and pains that come with life.

Thank you, Mom and Dad.

And thank you, Jesus.

"Always be joyful. Never stop praying. Be thankful in all circumstances, **for this is God's will for you** who belong to Christ Jesus."

—1 Thessalonians 5:16-18, NLT

While Paul doesn't specifically suggest bringing prayer into a marital bed, it seems like a great idea, doesn't it? You'll be hard-pressed to find a location that offers better potential for a mix of joy, prayer, and thankfulness.

What if you and your spouse found a way, however messy and brief, to give it a try? Or maybe the prayer happens in the bathroom when you're both brushing your teeth, just before you both leave for the day, or while you're washing the dinner dishes. It doesn't have to be pretty—just find a way to pray together today. Then give it another try tomorrow, and see what happens.

Giving Up on a Dream

I'd never paid much attention to the Bible story about Jacob, Esau, and the bowl of stew (Genesis 25:19-34). On the surface it seemed like one of those funny "what was he thinking?" stories from the Old Testament. But then something happened in my marriage that made me understand Esau a lot better.

My husband and I had been married about six years when it became increasingly clear that we wanted different things for our future. I was a musician and aspired to take my career to the next level. He was a wilderness enthusiast and wanted to spend more time in remote wilderness areas. Well, to be successful in music I needed connections and opportunities for gigs, and those happen in big musical cities like Los Angeles and Nashville, cities that aren't known for their wilderness adventures.

We both had jobs that we liked well enough in the town we lived in, so I couldn't really complain. It's just that I'd had this dream of playing music since I was a kid. It was a part of me, and I was antsy and disgruntled because of our inability to compromise on where to live.

"It's not like he didn't know this about me when we got married," I'd argue to myself. And I was right: He had known about my dream. He just wanted me to pursue it where we were so that he could be closer to his dream, too. The tension between us was causing more and more arguments, and I was discouraged.

One day I took a blanket and my Bible to the park to pray about the whole thing. I opened my Bible to a random page, hoping for inspiration. I landed on the story of Jacob tricking his famished brother, Esau, into trading his birthright for a bowl of stew. Thinking it inapplicable, I prepared to flip to something else when I heard Jesus' voice.

In one of the clearest warnings I'd ever heard from him, Jesus said, "Don't trade your birthright for a bowl of stew."

His words pierced my heart. I knew immediately what he meant. He was suggesting that in my desperation to achieve my dream, I was in danger of trading my future inheritance for a momentary need.

About this same time, one of my friends was talking about how God loves us enough to say no to the thing we want now because he's saying yes to the thing that's good for us 12 years from now. Or 20 years from now. Or 40.

It was the message of Esau all over again.

I was humbled. I'd been letting resentment against my husband grow for several years, feeling he was the one keeping me from my dream. I wanted him to be more flexible. I wanted God to change his mind and his heart so that we could move forward. But I was being challenged to take a step back and consider that God had a different plan with a different timeline. Maybe it was I who needed to change.

It's taken me a long time to come to terms with the fact that I may never achieve my childhood dream. But over time, my heart has opened to the possibility that there are other dreams—dreams my husband and I can share—that can bring me equal joy, just in different ways. I'm not sure what my "birthright" includes, but when I said yes to my husband and my marriage, I was saying yes to it, and it includes him. It's been hard to pass on the bowl of stew, but I'm believing that the inheritance down the road is infinitely more valuable.

J.

" 'For I know the plans I have for you,'
declares the Lord, **'plans to prosper
you, and not to harm you, plans to
give you hope and a future.' "**

—Jeremiah 29:11

Why do we have dreams, some that seem planted in us
by God, that must be sacrificed? How have you discerned
between a dream Jesus has given you to pursue and a
dream you need to see as "stew"? How have you seen him
love you "20 years from now" by doing something that was
hard for you in the short term? Stop for a moment and
ask Jesus to show you a dream that you and your spouse
can pursue *together*.

Three Cords

We finally bought a house!

Two inspectors had signed off on it; the closing went off without a hitch; it was ours.

And it was perfect: lots of sunlight streaming through the windows, lots of warm touches. It felt like home the day we moved in, and we were so grateful for it.

Then one evening within a week of moving in, we were watching TV when our cat strolled nonchalantly by carrying something in his mouth. Curious, we investigated and, after a game of Hide-and-Seek worthy of a sitcom, pried the object from his mouth.

It was a chunk of baseboard.

Huh.

Worried that our cat might have swallowed a nail, we went in search of the gap in the baseboard. At first we were relieved to find no missing nails. But wait. There were no missing nails because *there had never been any nails*. The baseboard wasn't nailed to the wall. It wasn't glued. It was simply leaning against the wall, and that was it. And this was true of not just one stretch of baseboard along one wall. Most of the baseboard throughout the entire house was just leaning in place.

Well, that was just…weird.

Later that week when my husband tried to slide open a window, it fell out of the opening. Just fell out. That's because it wasn't resting on a track; there was no track.

And then one morning as I was standing in the shower, I turned the hot and cold water handles, and they fell off in my hands. Good morning to you, too.

After that it seemed that everything we touched in that house leaked, fell down, or disintegrated. It was a disaster. Our dream had turned into a nightmare.

We endured a lawsuit that dragged on for years. Lawyers' fees ate up our savings until finally we were living from paycheck to paycheck. Our bank account was so depleted that we were in real danger of losing the house altogether.

When all of this started, we'd been married for five years. From the beginning of our married life, we had vowed not to turn into one of those couples who are always sniping at each other, and we'd kept that vow.

So that five years later, when the house nearly came crashing down around our heads, we had established a pattern of civility, of talking things over, of being fair and loving. We rarely fought; we genuinely viewed disagreements as opportunities to achieve deeper levels of understanding. And it worked. That foundation allowed us to weather the storm brought on by the house.

Our mantra became "Two are stronger than one."

So I can honestly say that the disaster known as the house actually brought us closer together.

But also during those first five years of our marriage, I'd been praying that my husband would develop a deeper, more personal relationship with Jesus.

The disaster known as the house did that, too.

One day, after learning of yet another court delay, my husband, Simon, broke down. He cried, "Why is this happening to us? I don't understand what we did to deserve this."

And then he asked me to pray. "Sure," I said, planning to talk privately with God the next time I had a few spare minutes.

Simon said, "No, I mean right now. With me. Would you pray with me?"

Until that moment, we had never prayed together.

And then, sitting at the kitchen counter, we did. I prayed first; then he prayed. We said "amen." Then he told me how thankful he was for me.

And that began a new, richer, deeper phase of our marriage. Now we pray together often. We read devotionals together. When we have guests, Simon prays before meals, and often he gets choked up, right there in front of God and everybody.

And all because our cat carried away a piece of baseboard.

"A cord of **three strands is not quickly broken.**"

—Ecclesiastes 4:12

In the Old Testament story of Joseph and his conniving brothers, the long-lost brother tells his now-repentant brothers: "You intended to harm me, but God intended it for good to accomplish what is now being done" (Genesis 50:20). Likewise, Jesus makes beauty out of ugliness—it's like breathing for him. What's something ugly in your life that you've seen him turn into something beautiful? Stop for a moment and thank him.

This week, braid three strands of yarn or twine into a bracelet and wear it as a tangible reminder that you, your spouse, and Jesus are all in your marriage together.

Does God Need Help?

"I want to be perfectly clear here: I don't want to have anything to do with God. I don't believe he exists. I'm done with him."

These were the words my husband—my *Christian* husband—said to me several months ago. Hearing him confess serious doubts and anger toward God was heartbreaking, disappointing, and frightening. "What if his faith doesn't recover?" I anguished. "What if he spends eternity apart from God?"

His comments frequently provoked me to argue apologetics with him. Every time he'd say something negative or false about God, I'd jump in to defend the God I love and follow. Usually these debates ended with me in tears and my husband more determined to resist God. Frustrated, I started praying more diligently for help in bringing my husband back to God.

Then one night I had a dream that completely changed my perspective about my role in shaping my husband's faith. In this dream I was in heaven enjoying what I can only describe as a "spa day." I spent the whole day being pampered, and at the very end I was ushered into God's throne room. When I walked into the room, I was surprised to see that my husband and God were wrapping up a conversation. Smiling, I walked up to them.

"What are you talking about?" I asked.

God smiled and said kindly, "That's none of your business."

Oh.

I woke up, the dream freshly imprinted on my mind. The meaning couldn't have been more definite. God's relationship with my husband includes things shared only between them. You'd think this knowledge would have made me feel left out. Instead, I was surprised and relieved. I'd taken on the responsibility of reconciling my husband with God. The dream reminded me that God can defend himself and that salvation is the work of the Holy Spirit, not of a distraught wife.

So how did this new perspective change the dynamics of our marriage? Well, I started keeping my emotions—fear, concern, disapproval, anger—to myself whenever my husband shared his doubts and frustrations. God doesn't need my indignation nearly as much as my trust, so I stopped being offended on his behalf.

I also stopped arguing apologetics with my husband. His attitude toward God isn't *right*, but his feelings are real. I can't just discount them because I disagree. So instead of preaching, arguing, pleading, and reasoning, I switched to two things: praying and listening.

I'm not sure what it will take to reconcile my husband with God, but I'm quite sure that God doesn't abandon the work he starts in us. And because it's *his* work, he asks for my trust, if not always my help.

"Being confident of this, that **he who began a good work in you will carry it on to completion** until the day of Christ Jesus."

—Philippians 1:6

On a scale of 1 to 10 (with 1 being "very upset" and 10 being "completely satisfied"), how happy are you with your spouse's relationship with God? In what ways do you sometimes "over-function" for your spouse, trying to troubleshoot his or her relationship with God because you're afraid? What's something you can start doing instead, and what's something you can stop doing? Jot down your thoughts here...

Porn

We were sitting in a restaurant with a group of friends from church. I picked up my husband's phone to look up something on the internet, and when I opened the browser, I felt as if I'd been kicked in the stomach. It was a porn site. My husband had been looking at porn.

I sat in stony silence during the ride home. He apologized, said he knew it was wrong.

But I couldn't un-see the image that had flashed in front of me on his phone. He had gone to someone outside of our marriage for sexual gratification.

To me, it was cheating. It was adultery.

And the sense of betrayal, the sense of being violated, wouldn't go away.

Although he'd always been accepting of my body, I couldn't help feeling that he was comparing me to the women on that site. Each time I lay next to him in bed, I felt the presence of a third person, someone he'd invited.

But if I was being really honest with myself, I had to admit that I hadn't been holding up my end of the bargain when it came to sex. I was never as interested in sex as I knew I should be. And I had to figure out why.

And that's where Jesus came in.

For a while, I'd been edging closer to understanding what it means to have a relationship with Jesus. I mean a real, interactive one. I had always thought it was possible for others to have that kind of relationship with him, but I figured it would never happen to me. I thought that sort of thing was reserved for the super-spiritual, not for me. I was too flawed, too broken.

But gradually I began to understand that all I really had to do was start listening for that "still, small voice." I began to be intentional about taking the time to be alone with Jesus.

I began to learn to quiet my mind. To get over myself. To stop demanding control. To stop the monologue that I used to think of as prayer. To listen to what Jesus might be wanting to say to me.

So it happened. I started to hear his voice. And it is *awesome* (the most overused word in our culture, but in this case, utterly apt).

I began to know: Jesus wanted me to get over my issues and become the wife he intended me to be.

So, without doing too much damage, I had to look those issues square in the eye. I had to take stock of how my past had affected my present.

I had to recognize that the sexual abuse I had suffered at the hands of a family member when I was a child had contaminated my view of myself and of sex.

I began to realize that my passive refusal to meet my husband's sexual needs was eroding his sense of self-worth and our marriage.

Just as I would be devastated if he refused to meet my emotional needs, to smile into my eyes and mean it, I was devastating him every time I signaled that I wasn't interested in sex.

And that broke my heart.

Finally, I realized that I need to pray for him, for whatever his issues are. I need to do this as his *friend* as well as his wife. I realized I'd been taking on his issues, adding them to my own. It was unbelievably freeing to realize that not everything is about me. That, in fact, God is in charge.

Marriage—and life—are so much easier now that I've stopped working so hard to control them. God is on his throne; Jesus is at his side; his Spirit dwells within me.

I'm free to be the woman, the wife, God created me to be.

"You may **love** the Lord your God, **listen** to his voice, and **hold fast** to him."

—Deuteronomy 30:20

Most of us tend to search for Jesus, to try to hear his voice, when we're desperate. Maybe we have to be headed toward the end of our rope before we really *believe*. And belief, according to Jesus, is the key to everything. So today, make a tiny investment in belief. What's something you can talk to Jesus about that you normally wouldn't? Share that with him right now, and then believe, like a little child, that he's going to respond.

The Living Word of God

My plan was simple: Get married, start trying to get pregnant on our second anniversary, and a year later—when my husband had just finished graduate school—we'd have our first child.

As plans go, it was an epic failure.

Infertility derailed the pregnancy I'd assumed would be no problem. And with the test results came devastating news: The medical issues were mine. All mine. I was the one preventing my dream from becoming a reality.

We adopted two children and became the family I'd always wanted.

Imagine our surprise when after 11 years of marriage my flu symptoms turned out to be something else. Something a whole lot better.

Reaction to the news of our pregnancy was overwhelming, an outpouring of enthusiasm. "It's such a miracle!" "What an answer to prayer!" "Such a blessing!"

And I agreed wholeheartedly.

But in my 34th week, I developed preeclampsia, a life-threatening condition. My health deteriorated quickly, and my husband and I were given a choice: an immediate emergency C-section or running the very real risk that I would die.

We were assured that 95 percent of babies delivered at 34 weeks do fine, so within hours our tiny son, Adam Anthony, came into the world.

A routine heart surgery—routine for preemies, at least—and an incubator in the neonatal intensive care unit, and Adam was on his way to a healthy life... until he wasn't.

A tired doctor, his brow creased with worry, delivered the grim news: Adam wasn't holding his own. Perhaps he wouldn't be among the 95 percent after all. And given Adam's condition, we needed to get to the unit as quickly as possible.

We were escorted to a "grieving room," and our son's incubator was wheeled in. Adam was gently placed in our arms. We spoke to him, prayed for him, wrapped his tiny hands in ours.

And our son, our Adam, died as we held him close.

I cried. I struggled. I wanted Jesus to explain what we had done to deserve this, to be given such a blessing only to have it yanked away from us.

A support group helped, as did hugs and counseling. But it wasn't nearly enough.

What pulled me to safety from the deep waters of grief was reading Jesus' words in the Bible. I met him there in passages I'd read often, but never while nursing a shattered heart.

I let his words soothe my soul, refresh my spirit.

His words of life. His words of joy.

His words for me.

"So also **you have sorrow now, but** I will see you again, and **your hearts will rejoice, and no one will take your joy** from you."

—John 16:22, ESV

As Jesus prepared his followers for difficult days ahead, he didn't give them a pep talk or ask that they hang tough. He didn't shame them for the worry in their eyes.

Instead he pointed them to himself because *that's* where they'd find hope…and healing…and joy.

Where in your life do you need hope or help or joy? Journal your answers to that question below, and then tell Jesus, "I need to hear your words right now. Please flash a Gospel reference (Matthew, Mark, Luke, or John—plus a chapter number and verse number) in my head. I'll go there and receive whatever I find as from you." Write what you discover and how it might relate to your present situation here…

Details

Y ou know how when you first fall in love with someone, you notice every little detail? For instance, I was struck by the color of my husband's eyes: deep blue, except when he wore certain shirts that turned them electric blue.

We've been married 10 years, and I confess that I haven't noticed the color of his eyes in a long time. Over the years he's just became so *familiar*. His habits, his routines, the things he talks about, his moods, the way he looks—I've seen and heard them all thousands of times; I don't even notice them anymore.

I suppose this is normal, but recently the Holy Spirit started talking to me about how I don't even notice *my husband* anymore. I mean, *really* notice him. The other morning, for instance, I was sitting in the kitchen, and he was talking about an issue that'd come up at work. I listened to maybe a quarter of his words, just enough to nod intelligently and repeat phrases if needed. Just enough to *fake* attention without really giving it.

I don't do this maliciously. I love this man, I swear. I treasure his heart and his ideas. But my head is so full of my own thoughts that I'm perpetually distracted. Other times I can predict what he's going to say, and I've already moved on by the time he gets there.

"You're missing so much," the Spirit keeps whispering to me. "What if you really, *truly* paid attention to him? What would that look like?"

I'm sure you'd answer this question differently, but in the past whenever I needed to really pay attention, I took notes. I figured it wouldn't hurt in my marriage, so to help me pay attention, I started keeping a notebook. In it, I wrote down answers to questions like "What was he really animated about today? Why does he care so much about that?" and "What did he say that was skipped over but could be revisited?" and "How did he look, anyway? What was his mood? What story were his eyes telling?"

(I actually tried taking notes while he was talking, but he thought that was really weird, so I had to stop.)

This approach may be too clinical for your marriage; I'm sure Jesus has other ideas for other couples. I just know that my husband is the most important person in my life and he deserves more than distracted half-listening. He deserves someone who notices his beautiful blue eyes.

"Do nothing out of selfish ambition or vain conceit. Rather, **in humility value others above yourselves,** not looking to your own interests but each of you to the interests of the others."

—Philippians 2:3-4

In your next conversation with your spouse, pay ridiculous attention to him or her. Then ask Jesus, "What have I been missing about my spouse?" In the space below, journal what emerges from this experiment. Then ask Jesus for help in paying better attention to your spouse.

_____

_____

_____

_____

_____

_____

_____

_____

Infidelity

We had a beautiful church wedding, a lovely swirl of flowers and lace, delicate decorations, and a bright, shining future. Craig and I stood before smiling friends and family to exchange rings, vowing to be faithful until death separated us.

When we launched into our life together, I didn't know how quickly or thoroughly it could be shattered.

Infidelity leaves nothing but destruction in its wake. When my husband decided he loved another woman and walked out of our home, he swept away the foundation of our life together. I was left staggering, wanting our marriage to survive but unsure how that could possibly happen.

Jesus quickly became the only thing—the only person—I could fully trust. People might betray me. But Jesus? Never.

And I turned to the church, knowing if there was any place I could find the truth about my situation, it was the church. If there was any place I'd find a way to mend what was broken in my marriage, it was the church.

But instead, one Sunday morning the minister suggested that some of us in the congregation needed to break free from our wedding vows. He stepped out from behind the pulpit and swept an inviting arm toward the stage. If we needed Jesus' power to break free from the bondage of unhealthy marriages, he invited us forward so we could ask Jesus for help.

I didn't walk forward, but I knew I couldn't stay where I was, either. I needed resolution: divorce or restoration. Staying forever in no man's land wasn't an option. So I asked Jesus what I should do. I told him if he made it clear which direction I should go, I was willing to follow.

A few days later I received a call at my office from Craig's mistress. She'd phoned to tell me about the two of them. She thought I should know.

When I hung up, I whispered a prayer thanking Jesus for providing the direction I'd wanted—and a growing peace about pursuing divorce. I began planning to end the marriage I'd thought would last forever.

A few weeks later, as I was about to leave my office, I glanced up, and standing in the doorway was the last person I expected to see: Craig.

He walked over to me and took both my hands in his.

He told me he'd talked with his "friend" and ended the relationship. Then he asked if he could pray with me, something he'd never asked to do with me before.

Had Craig said anything else—anything—I'm not sure if I'd have listened. But who was I to refuse to pray?

He spoke words of sincere repentance, and when he finished praying, I looked up through tears to see the same soft eyes I'd seen when I'd given my heart to Craig years before.

And I could sense Jesus telling me—telling us—to trust him. It would be Jesus, and not divorce attorneys, who would write the last chapter of our story.

Easy? No. Forgiveness and rebuilding trust never are. But a year later we renewed our vows and once again invited Jesus to join us together.

Craig and I are now in our second marriage together, and we're determined not to take our eyes off Jesus. Because it's only Jesus who can guide us to the happily-ever-after we wanted from the start.

"If you forgive other people when they sin against you, your heavenly Father will also forgive you."

—Matthew 6:14

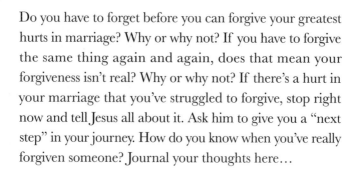

Do you have to forget before you can forgive your greatest hurts in marriage? Why or why not? If you have to forgive the same thing again and again, does that mean your forgiveness isn't real? Why or why not? If there's a hurt in your marriage that you've struggled to forgive, stop right now and tell Jesus all about it. Ask him to give you a "next step" in your journey. How do you know when you've really forgiven someone? Journal your thoughts here…

_____

_____

_____

_____

Letting Mistakes Happen

I could see where this was headed. My wife was hunkered down at the kitchen table planning a party for friends and family. Cookbooks were spread out everywhere, and she'd made stacks of notes. She'd already asked for my opinion about what kind of dip goes best with something called crudités, and ever since then I'd been diligently avoiding the kitchen. But now it was 2:00 in the afternoon, and my stomach was growling for an overdue lunch.

"Oh, hey. How many people do you think we can fit into the dining room? If we pushed the sofas against the wall, do you think we could extend a table into the other room?"

"Whatever you want," I replied, dodging the question. I'd watched her go down this road so many times. She was always trying to create the perfect get-togethers, and in the process, she'd try to do too much and spend too much money. And each time the event would end up disappointing her.

"You really think they'll fit?" she persisted.

I held my tongue and nodded, concentrating on my sandwich. I was practicing something our marriage counselor had suggested to me, which was to let her make her own mistakes without always trying to prevent them from happening. The idea sat uncomfortably with me, but after I'd prayed about it, God reminded me how many mistakes he'd let me make and how much I'd learned from them. "It feels like helping, but you're actually holding her back," he said.

I knew the party wouldn't go well, but because I was trying to resist my habit of problem-solving with her, I didn't mention that her menu was way too complicated or suggest that she pad her schedule with another three weeks for planning. "She has to make her own mistakes," I kept reminding myself.

As predicted, the party was a disaster. She waited until the last minute to shop and prepare food, and on the night of the party she was running around the kitchen like a maniac. There were some oven casualties that filled the house with smoke about 20 minutes before people arrived. And then, as she was frantically trying to make everything perfect, she started snapping orders at people. It wasn't pretty.

Afterward, I found her slumped in the empty kitchen, a stack of dirty dishes in the sink, tears on her cheeks. "I totally overdid it," she moaned. "I waited too long to get started and then was so exhausted and stressed that I wasn't even nice to people."

"What do you think you could do differently next time?" I asked.

"Oh, lots of things," she replied. "But probably the first thing is that I need to quit trying so hard to make my friends like me."

What followed was a good conversation about why her friends make her feel insecure, and I got a chance to encourage her rather than try to fix her mistakes before they happen. We both ended the evening by doing the dishes together, and I had a chance to thank God for accomplishing through her mistakes what I hadn't been able to accomplish by helping her.

"And we know that **in all things God works for the good of those who love him**, who have been called according to his purpose."

—Romans 8:28

The impulse to protect and rescue our spouses is strong but can sometimes hold them back. How are you protecting your spouse from making mistakes? What prevents you from letting go of your need to intervene? When you're alone, cup your hands together in front of your face and imagine you're holding your spouse in them. Then lift your cupped hands above your head and offer your spouse to Jesus. Entrust him or her to Jesus' care and concern. Bring your hands back down separately, as a symbol that you've given the caretaking of your spouse to Jesus.

Honesty

For a few years after we married, my wife, Shandra, consistently interrupted me to finish my sentences.

At first it was sort of charming. I'd start a sentence, she'd finish it, and then we'd gaze into each other's eyes, marveling at how perfectly in sync we were.

Except by year three it was driving me insane.

I'd be thinking about how to navigate Christmas and make the mistake of pausing, just a nanosecond, as I collected my thoughts.

Me: "Hey, sweetie, I was thinking that this Christmas it might be good if…"

Shandra: "…we visited my mom and dad. Thanks, honey!"

Me (thinking): *…we stayed home and hung out together without your dopey brothers and strange Uncle Larry around.*

Me (talking): "Um…you're welcome?"

But the thing is, I couldn't really blame Shandra. I hadn't been honest with her. When she finished my sentences, she was often wrong, but I never told her. And since I hadn't said anything early on, how could I complain later?

I should have done what Jesus was calling me to do: Be honest and transparent. All the stuff we'd promised to be when Shandra and I married. The stuff that, as Jesus-followers, we knew was needed to both serve him and be true to each other.

It's called *integrity*, and as Jesus was working on me to take mine more seriously, I could see what *not* having integrity had done in my marriage.

By not risking a hard conversation in the moment, I'd set Shandra and me up for an even harder one down the road. I'd lied by omission, and I'd lied so thoroughly that she thought I was joking when I finally confessed the truth Jesus was nudging me to share.

She arched an eyebrow and said, "You know, I can finish your sentences for you because you're so…predictable."

Predictable? *Me?* No way could I let *that* stand. I forgot all about Jesus and integrity and set about proving I was anything but predictable.

My solution? I got a tattoo. It's an arrow on my ankle with the words "This end up."

I'll admit it's one lame tattoo, but for a needle-hating guy to walk into a tattoo parlor and plunk down cash to be jabbed repeatedly, that *was* unpredictable.

When Shandra noticed my bandaged ankle and asked what happened, I told her I'd gotten a tattoo. She didn't believe me.

Perfect! I showed her!

And then I realized that I'd missed the point. Completely. Jesus was pointing me toward fixing what was out of whack in my marriage by having a conversation, and I'd gotten tattooed instead.

Shandra and I still shake our heads about how that all played out. I'm still walking around with tattooed evidence of what not risking an honest conversation can lead to in a marriage.

And Shandra, well…she mostly can't quite believe she married a guy who could get things so wrong.

But on the plus side there's this: She no longer finishes my sentences.

"Instead, we will **speak the truth in love, growing** in every way more and **more like Christ**, who is the head of his body, the church."

—Ephesians 4:15, NLT

Speaking the truth in love is a balancing act. It's being direct without being destructive, being clear without being condemning. And it requires you to bathe every word in love.

But our definition of *love* is directly tied to the things Jesus said and did, and Jesus loved people all along the scale from tenderness to bluntness. What's one way you've avoided loving your spouse because it would require you to do something tough? Journal your answer below. Then ask Jesus, simply, "What do you want me to do about this?" Wait in silence for him to respond, and then journal what you "get" in the space below.

Scapegoat

I sat at the top of the stairs looking down at him as he paced the floor below, fists clenched and face red.

I honestly can't remember why he was angry. But it seemed we'd already had this fight 12 times that week. His temper was a land mine, and no matter how cautiously I stepped, I kept setting him off.

"Don't react," I coached myself. "That's what he wants. It's only been a couple of months."

I thought back over the past few weeks. It was a Tuesday when his mom called to tell us that his dad had died. We'd been expecting it, of course; he'd been sick for a while. But still, the news was devastating. We'd spent the first couple of weeks going through the motions—the funeral, the burial, the usual condolences. We'd had so many close moments, remembering his dad together, our hearts full of joy for his life and joy for each other in the midst of grief. In a weird way, it seemed his dad's death had brought us closer as a couple. Closer than we'd been in a long time, actually.

And then one day I woke up, and the closeness was gone. In its place was Land Mine Man. Easily provoked, my husband was surly, mean-spirited, and short-tempered. And I was his target. Everything I did annoyed him. Everything triggered an argument. We began rehashing disagreements I thought we'd settled years before. He even mentioned divorce.

He was still pacing and yelling at the foot of the stairs. A weary sigh escaped me as I cradled my head in my hands. I'd been so patient, but I couldn't help it—I burst into tears, suddenly realizing why I was really upset. It wasn't the arguments and insults. It was that I'd just had the sweetest couple of weeks with him—full of affection, kindness, and love—and I hadn't realized how thirsty my heart was for his full attention until I lost it again.

It was then that I snapped.

All the insults and arguments and attacks, all the disappointment, imploded. I'd had enough. Standing, I spat a few choice words in his face, turned, and stomped to my room, slamming the door behind me.

"How dare he continue to attack me!" I ranted to Jesus. "Any fool can see that he's taking his grief out on me. I don't deserve this, and it's not fair to be treated this way. I will not allow him to use me as his scapegoat."

Pausing to catch my breath, I heard him, the quiet voice of Jesus whispering right to my heart.

"I was the scapegoat," he said.

Instantly my blaze of rage was snuffed out. Of course I didn't deserve to be treated this way. Of course I had every right to stand up for myself. My husband was wrong. And yet none of that mattered. I would let him take his grief out on me even though it wasn't fair. Even though it cost me something. I would be the scapegoat because Jesus was the scapegoat. The decision was easy, like breathing.

I don't remember how the rest of the evening went. I know that eventually I came out of the room and we moved on. The weeks and months that followed held more arguments and hurts, but they'd lost much of their potency. That night changed me—and him. My decision to be like Jesus broke something, and we gradually moved closer to each other again, affection and kindness growing from the ground where land mines used to be.

The choice to be a scapegoat goes against every instinct. It's unjust for the innocent to bear someone else's wrongdoing. And yet, as in so many other times in my marriage, Jesus asked me to do the counterintuitive thing, and then he helped me carry it through. These moments of zigging when zagging was clearly the just thing to do have had the greatest impact on my marriage. All they require is listening and a willingness to obey. Jesus does the rest.

"**You were redeemed**…with the precious blood of Christ, a lamb without blemish or defect."

—1 Peter 1:18-19

It's natural and right to want to be treated fairly by a spouse, yet sometimes Jesus asks us to sacrifice what we deserve in order to achieve something greater. Is there anything you're hanging on to because you feel you deserve it, that it's rightfully yours? Stop for a moment and ask Jesus to help you let go of it.

Divorce

It was 2:00 a.m. when a persistent doorbell rattled me awake. One look at Jackie told me everything I needed to know.

"Don't answer it," she said, sliding up on one elbow on the far side of the bed.

But I padded down the dark stairs and pulled open our front door to an icy January night.

And someone I didn't want to see.

Finding out Jackie was having an affair had been hell. But lies, stray phone calls, and late-night emergencies at the office had all added up. And after a flurry of indignant denials, she'd at last confessed and promised it was over, that she was serious this time about fixing what was broken in our marriage.

She'd even agreed to couples counseling and, after a false start or two, had more or less shown up for our weekly appointments.

But standing on the porch at 2:00 a.m., a bit drunk and a lot insistent, was the Other Guy.

He'd come, he said, to "settle things." He loved my wife, they were still seeing each other, and she wasn't happy with me. So it was time to sort out the details.

Turns out Jackie *hadn't* broken off her affair.

She'd lied—again. And again. And again.

Betrayal is devastating. Betrayal with a side order of coverup is worse, leaving no oxygen to keep hope and trust alive. If you can't believe your spouse—your *Christian* spouse—who *can* you believe?

I decided the answer was: no one. Not women. Not acquaintances who'd known but said nothing. Not even Jesus who, as best I could tell, hadn't shown up with some thunderclap of healing.

Except he *did* come by, wrapped in the skin of friends.

There was Mark, who promised to walk with me through the divorce and the next few years. And Terry, whose encouragement never faltered. Gerard and Donna, Mary and Tom. Men and women who stepped up and into my messy life in ways that literally saved it.

Sometimes marriages don't go the distance; that's a sad fact.

But I've realized that Jesus' love does, if you recognize it for what it is and cling to it.

I'd counted on Jesus to provide a counseling breakthrough, a flash of insight that would bring Jackie and me back together. Never happened. Instead, he sent his people with hugs, prayers, and promises (all kept) to *be there no matter what.*

"**Every good and perfect gift is from above,** coming down **from the Father of the heavenly lights**, **who does not change** like shifting shadows."

—James 1:17

Jesus is reaching out to you somehow, right now. Whether you're experiencing hurt, anger, or perhaps even joy in your marriage, Jesus is with you and loving you. That's simply who he is.

The question is this: Do you recognize how he's reaching out? It may not be in ways you're expecting.

How is Jesus reaching out to you as you navigate your marriage? And here's a hint about where to look: Where are you feeling most whole and hopeful today? Journal your response.

Jesus, the Namer

It was early in my marriage. I was a featured speaker at a big ministry conference, the last place I wanted to be at that moment in my life. The arguments that were typical of our early marriage had escalated into a cycle of wounding. We were both prisoners of our broken identities. I believed there was a hollow place where my soul should've been, and that belief was destroying our love for each other. When I left our home for the conference, Bev's icy silence frightened me. I could tell what had just happened between us was way beyond our typical patterns of recovery and forgiveness followed by a slow thaw. As I boarded the plane, I felt like I was standing in the queue for the electric chair and would have given anything for a hint of mercy. I arrived at the hotel and immediately found a quiet place to call her. She answered, heard my voice, and hung up. I did this repeatedly, like a man insane. Every abrupt end to my call was like a dagger jammed and twisted into my gut.

So I walked through the halls of the convention center dazed, hoping no one would recognize me so I wouldn't have to muster the required cheerfulness. I crept close to the walls, afraid to show myself. The voices inside me were thick with accusation and criticism. It was during one of these journeys down a crowded hallway that I felt Jesus beckoning me. If he had suddenly appeared before me, I wouldn't have been surprised—his voice was so urgent and magnetic. I looked around for someplace to "meet" him, and an unlocked door led me to a darkened, empty conference room. I had a legal pad and a pen with me, so I sat on the floor with the pad on my lap, waiting. And then his voice came like a thunderstorm. I had to write fast just to keep up. I didn't even process what he said while I wrote; the "transcription" was all I could handle at first. And then, when I read it for the first time, it was as if paramedics had jolted me with those electrified paddles that kick-start your heart.

He did nothing to fix my fears or promise an easy reconciliation; instead, he described what was there in that hollow place where my soul was supposed to be, using a metaphorical name for me that is so deeply intimate that it still brings tears to my eyes as I type these words. Here's what I transcribed:

You're a quarterback. You see the field. You're squirming away from the rush to find space to release the ball. You never give up. You have courage in the face of ferocity; in fact, ferocity draws out your courage. You want to score even when the team is too far behind for it to matter. You love the thrill of creating a play in the huddle, under pressure, and spreading the ball around to everyone on the team. You have no greater feeling than throwing the ball hard to a spot and watching the receiver get to it without breaking stride. In fact, you love it most when the receiver is closely covered and it takes a perfect throw to get it to him. You have the same feeling when you throw a bomb and watch the receiver run under it, or when you tear away from the grasp of a defender, or when you see and feel blood on your elbows or knees and feel alive because of it. You love to score right after the other team has scored, but you want to do it methodically, first down by first down, right down the field. You love fourth down! You want to win but are satisfied by fighting well.

I felt as if I'd been yanked out of the torrent. I cried and cried and cried until I couldn't cry anymore. At my most desperate hour, the Lord Jesus saved me by naming me. He marked my identity with truth and gave me a hope that was not dependent on a happy ending to my crisis. While "Rick" sums up my history, "Quarterback" sums up my nature, the truth about my heart and identity. Jesus never uses duct tape to fix things; he'll take your flesh and blood if you offer it to him and use it like clay.

When I returned home, my wife stood a few feet from me and spoke from a thousand miles away—she asked for a separation. "I'd like you out of the house by tonight." I moved into the basement apartment of a co-worker, and later the basement apartment of a friend. I spent the holidays apart from her, crying all the time as the husk of the false identity I'd worn my whole life loosened and fell away. I reminded myself of "Quarterback" as I lay down on the threshing floor, helpless to stop the pounding, holding on to Jesus like a shipwrecked man clings to the only piece of floating wreckage he can find.

And then, a few months later, in the middle of an appointment with our counselor, Carl, the husk finally fell away. One moment I was describing the emptiness that was "Rick" before my naming experience at the conference, and the next I was bursting into uncontrollable, soul-shaking sobs as Carl bolted across the room to kneel in front of me, his face just inches from mine, his eyes locked on mine. "Rick, your soul is full, and you are loved." These words uncorked something primal in me. I rushed from the room like a man needing to vomit up the bile that had simmered in my soul for a quarter-century. I drove a few blocks away and parked by an empty field, where my sobs shook the car and I felt my first taste of freedom. I could barely walk after this experience. A few weeks later I moved back into our home and, like the parent of a newborn, started to get to know the truth about myself for the first time. And I discovered that finding my own name gave me the foundation and courage to name others.

"Quarterback" is no mere affirmation, just as a wedding is no mere date. Affirmation makes us feel good about who we are. Naming reveals our true nature. And the only one who knows what is *most true* about us is Jesus. In a world of distorted mirrors, his is the only one not marred and broken. We must have a deeper sense of our redeemed identity if we're to be a source of life and redemption in our marriages. Otherwise, we are always attempting to extract our identities from our spouses. We live with each other like leeches but don't know it. Jesus invites us to find ourselves in him. My friend Ned Erickson once shared "The Progression" with me, a perfect description of the way Jesus first draws us and then marks us...

"Get to know Jesus well, because the more you know him, the more you'll love him, and the more you love him, the more you'll want to follow him, and the more you follow him, the more you'll become like him, and the more you become like him, the more you become yourself."

"Behold, I will do a new thing,
now it shall spring forth;
shall you not know it?"

—Isaiah 43:19, NKJV

When we're struggling in our marriages, we're understandably desperate for Jesus to bring healing or resolution or a good outcome. Instead, ask Jesus, "Who do you say that I am?" Then wait in silence—however long it takes—to receive from him. Don't resist what comes with skepticism or unbelief; just receive it. Then tell someone you trust what Jesus has shown you, giving others a chance to confirm it or nuance it for you.

The Longest Nights

There it was again: that feeling in the pit of my stomach that he wasn't telling me everything. Something was just...off. I went to bed, and before falling asleep I found myself praying this prayer: "Jesus, I'm tired of being in the dark. I'm tired of being surprised. I'm tired of this process of getting to the truth, one layer at a time, like we're peeling an onion. I just want to know it all, even if it's too much to deal with. I want the whole truth."

I woke up early the next morning with a feeling that I should check my husband's phone. What surfaced was far, far worse than I'd imagined. He'd been lying to me for years, covering things up. Even when we were in counseling and I thought we were making progress, he was only sharing part of the truth. And what he was covering up was big stuff. Like divorce-big stuff. Deal-breaker stuff. Illegal stuff. I didn't know how exposed I was, but I suspected it was bad. I changed the locks and closed accounts. I stopped eating and sleeping. Crying through the nights, I prepared for divorce.

It's hard for me to describe the long nights I spent sobbing on the floor. They were so dark that even now when I think of them, I shudder a little. But in the midst of the darkness, I never for one moment felt I had to rely on my own strength. I had none, so Jesus gave me a supernatural strength that I knew didn't come from myself. I felt complete surrender and total protection.

But this protection and surrender didn't shield me from my emotions. Grief. Anger. Betrayal. I felt all of them, like waves crashing over me. I wasn't doing well. I wasn't riding above the waves or being "content in Jesus" or (fill in any other clichés that spring to mind here). I was a total mess. The only thing I knew was that I wasn't going to go under.

Gradually, in the midst of the mess, Jesus started speaking "beauty out of ashes" to me. Other people confirmed the phrase to me in several different ways, which was so good because I knew I couldn't trust my own thoughts during that time. Even my husband started hearing it, like from strangers in the hardware store (seriously, that happened). I wasn't sure what it meant, but it gave me hope that God was working. It still seemed divorce was inevitable, but maybe "beauty out of ashes" meant that we could be healed after all, that healing had already begun.

Fast-forward to a year later, and we're still married. As it turned out, it took a few more weeks after my initial prayer for the full truth to emerge. Some of my initial fears turned out to be unfounded. We went back to counseling. We're still working through it, still getting to more truth.

I have to be honest: It's still scary. I feel like the bottom could drop out at any moment. But here's what gets me through: an unwavering confidence that no matter what happens, Jesus will keep my head above water. Even if I lose all my strength, he will give me supernatural protection just as he did during those first dark nights crying on the floor.

And I know that "beauty out of ashes" is a promise I can trust. I don't know how all of this will be resolved, but I have hope. Jesus can make all things—even the ugliest, scariest things—beautiful in his way. For me, beauty has already started to sprout in the midst of rubble.

J.

"**To all who mourn** in Israel, **he will give a crown of beauty for ashes, a joyous blessing instead of mourning, festive praise instead of despair**. In their righteousness, they will be like great oaks that the Lord has planted for his own glory."

—Isaiah 61:3, NLT

Jesus gives us not only supernatural strength to make it through the darkest of nights but also real hope. When Jesus has given you hope in your marriage, how has he delivered it? What does hope really mean to you, anyway? A good resolution to your challenges? How have you experienced hope apart from that outcome? How is hope infusing your perspective on your relationship with your spouse?

Finding the "Right One"

My request for marital help started way before I got married. I wanted Jesus' help in finding and marrying the right woman.

Trust me, I know what it is to end up with the wrong person. My dating life had been a string of train wrecks, and I'd begun wondering if the "right one" existed at all. And, if she did, how I'd recognize her.

My friends suggested a strategic shift. Rather than mope around, hoping to meet my future wife through friends or by chance, I could fast-track my search by joining Match.com and finding people who were interested in the same things I cared about.

I debated for a few months—should I join or not? Then, figuring I had nothing to lose, I plunked down my credit card for a three-month membership. I was diving in.

My first dinner date was with a woman whose profile I'd studied in depth. I asked her about those things in her profile I found intriguing, and she answered my questions…but with nothing more than the bare facts. When I finally asked what she'd found interesting in my profile, she paused, took a sip of water, and then said, "Nothing."

She'd hardly read it. This was her second date of the day, fourth in the past week. She just liked getting out, and this was a very nice restaurant and a free meal.

I called for the check, I walked her to her car, and she drove away. Probably to another date.

That weekend at church a married couple led the worship time. I sat watching them worship together and found myself wistfully wondering, *Will that ever happen for me?*

And then I heard it: "Dave, where you're looking isn't where she's going to be found."

Just like that. A voice. One I knew was Jesus'. And I was flooded with a warm assurance that Jesus was already coming alongside my marriage, even though I hadn't even met my wife yet.

Jesus was tilling the soil, preparing me for someone.

I deleted my dating profile and never looked at Match.com again. If the woman Jesus had in mind for me wasn't on the site, I wasn't going to waste my time there.

Though I still wondered how I'd notice if I ever ran into her.

That turned out not to be an issue because *she* ran into *me*...literally. Pulling out of a Starbucks, my truck was smacked by a car driven by a cute brunette who simply hadn't noticed me until it was too late to brake.

But *I* noticed *her*. And the best thing about an accident is that you exchange contact information... information I put to good use.

It didn't happen quickly, but that first collision turned into something more than swapping the names of our All State agents. It turned into a date... and then another date...and eventually we were back at that Starbucks.

Except this time I was down on one knee proposing to the Christian woman who stole my heart shortly after she totaled my truck.

She said yes.

"**My sheep listen to my voice**; I know them, **and they follow me**."

—John 10:27

If Jesus actually spoke to you about your current situation, would you know it's him? *How* would you know?

And then there's this: Do you typically act on what you hear? Why or why not?

Find a secluded spot and take a few deep breaths. Then, out loud, say this: "Jesus, I'm listening. What do you have to say to me about my marriage…my life…our friendship?"

Listen for a word. Wait for an image to come to mind. Let memories come to you. What might Jesus be whispering to you?

And now what, if anything, are you willing to do about it?

Two Approaches

My husband, Blake, is not a Christian. Several years ago, it became clear that he had a drinking problem. It had taken a long time for me to recognize this, and it took Blake even longer to acknowledge it. And even after we reached that point, there were lots of stops and starts in his journey toward sobriety. Two incidents during that time illustrate how I handled this on my own—relying on my own understanding— and how I handled it after I took my hands off the steering wheel and allowed Jesus to drive.

The first incident occurred after Blake had promised me that he had stopped drinking. We were at some friends' house for a large dinner party, and Blake and I were seated in different rooms. Afterward, as we were driving home, I asked, "Was it hard for you not to drink tonight?"

He replied, "Not really." I told him I was so proud of him for this act of self-discipline, and I was encouraged that he really had turned a corner.

The next day, I met with several friends with whom I get together once a week for prayer. Three of them were also at the dinner party the night before. When I told them how proud I was of Blake for not drinking, they looked at one another, looked at me, and then looked away. I asked, "What? What aren't you telling me?" Embarrassed, they told me that Blake had drunk three large glasses of red wine in quick succession the night before. I was embarrassed, hurt, disgusted, and angry.

When I got home, I confronted Blake, saying, "Why did you lie to me? Look, I'm not your priest. I'm not your mother. But you have a real problem, and you need to find a solution." I was certainly within my rights to say all of this, but my words, my attitude, and my demeanor infuriated Blake. That day we lost a lot of ground.

Several months passed. During that time, I learned to rely more and more on Jesus for direction and guidance, as none of my own tactics were working. I had come to realize that I could do nothing to affect positive change outside of God's Spirit working within me. And I had stopped having internal dialogues, imagining how conversations would evolve if I just said exactly the right thing in the right way at the right time. Instead, I continually asked God to allow me to see Blake through God's eyes, to soften my heart, to speak and act through me.

One evening before bedtime I surprised Blake in his office, a semidetached building next to our house. It was late, and he wasn't expecting me. When I walked in, he hurriedly put something in a cabinet, and I knew he'd been drinking. I said, "Honey, have you been drinking?"

He looked down, ashamed, and said, "Yes."

Without thinking, I said, "Oh, baby, what's going on?"

The air seemed to leave his body. He just crumpled and said, "I don't know. I don't know." He was so lost. We stood there, holding each other, for a long, long time. A great deal of ground was regained that evening. And it was because Jesus was at the helm, transforming my heart.

"Be kind and compassionate to one another, forgiving each other, just as in Christ God forgave you."

—Ephesians 4:32

What's the hardest thing about your spouse to "give to Jesus"? Ask Jesus to give you a soft and supple heart toward your spouse this week, to help you see your spouse through Jesus' eyes. Then write about the difference this has made.

Unpredictable

We were in a breakout session during a financial class, and I was sitting next to a young couple talking about managing debt. Fresh-faced and married for, like, a day, they were convinced they were set for smooth sailing.

I couldn't help smiling, remembering myself at their age. I knew something they didn't, which is that life is unpredictable.

Take me, for instance. At their age I was a financial broker, and I often met with couples who were carrying piles of debt.

"Those poor couples," I would think. "I'm so glad we'll never be in their position."

Famous last words.

My wife's anxiety started out slowly, but over the years it became harder and harder for her to manage. Eventually she lost her job, which wouldn't have been a big deal if I hadn't launched my business at about that same time.

What followed was a downward spiral of debt, increased anxiety, and arguments. Fortunately, the tide had finally turned, and we were pulling ourselves out of debt (hence the financial class).

Listening to the young couple talk about their plans, I wondered how the future would change them. My wife and I were regaining financial ground, but she'd emerged from the stress a different person. Her heart, once open and confident, was hard. Her faith, once strong, had faltered, creating a widening chasm between her and God.

One day as I was listening to a podcast, the host mentioned a verse that Paul had written about forgetting the past and looking to the future. His words resonated with me, and I knew in that moment that I had to let go of the past. My wife, whoever she was now, was the person God was calling me to love and serve. He wasn't asking me to love yesterday's version of her, but today's.

I'll admit that loving her now is more challenging. It requires more sacrifice, and sometimes the scales seem unfairly balanced in her favor, as I give more than she does. But God's love for us isn't fairly balanced either; it tips in our favor more than we deserve. This is the model of love we're called to follow, even if it costs us something. In fact, it's *supposed* to cost us something.

If I could tell that young couple at the class just one thing, I would tell them that in spite of whatever challenges they face, they can learn to love each other right where they are. That's what I'm trying to do.

"Brothers and sisters, I do not consider myself yet to have taken hold of it. But one thing I do: **Forgetting what is behind and straining toward what is ahead,** I press on **toward the goal to win the prize for which God has called me** heavenward in Christ Jesus."

—Philippians 3:13-14

How have life's unpredictable twists and turns changed you? How have they changed your spouse? Jesus told us that anyone can love the people who love them back but his "brand" of love involves loving our enemies. Talk about a "fairness imbalance"! What does it mean to you to love your spouse just as he or she is, even if he or she seems like an enemy right now? Ask Jesus for a next step in this, a simple act of faith and trust that finds a way to love your spouse just as he or she is today. Jot your thoughts in the space below.

Confronting the Boogeyman

My mom and I have a complicated relationship. For much of my childhood, she was one person in public and a very different person in the privacy of our home. The source of her split personality was her alcoholism, a condition she hid with relative effectiveness, except from those closest to her.

Alcoholism touches everything in a family. For instance, when I was a child, I could never predict what kind of mood she'd be in. Some days she was friendly, funny, and warm. Others she was distant and passive-aggressive, dolling out the silent treatment without explanation. Because of this, I never felt comfortable having friends over. Would they meet Friendly Mom or Silent-Treatment Mom? I couldn't be sure.

Of course her drinking affected my parent's marriage, placing a strain on it that my father handled with grace until eventually it was too much and they divorced. I was a young adult at the time and promised myself that whoever I married wouldn't be an alcoholic.

When I discovered a few years later that the husband I'd recently married had a drinking problem, I was filled with shame.

"How did I marry into this?" I thought. "How could I not have recognized the signs?"

I also wondered why God let me marry this man. I'd prayed fervently about whether I should marry him, and I'd felt confident that God blessed the marriage. So when the reality of my husband's drinking surfaced, I asked a lot of questions, like "Did I miss God's choice for me? Did I choose wrong? Will I be sentenced to a dysfunctional marriage like my parents'? Am I destined for divorce?"

One day over coffee I was sharing some of these questions with a friend I trusted because she seemed to hear God's voice so clearly. She looked at me and said, "You realize that your marriage is different from your parents', right? And that God is telling a different story through your life? I believe it's a hopeful story. I see a lot of love between you and your husband, and I see Jesus growing your faith and softening your heart during this process. Don't make drinking a boogeyman. Jesus can do surprising things."

Her words were like a breath of fresh air. I realized that from the minute I discovered my husband's drinking, I'd assumed we'd end up like my parents. But that wasn't fair—we were a different couple.

Even more, I knew my friend was right: There *was* a lot of love between my husband and me. And unlike my parents, we communicated well, even about his drinking. It wasn't fair of me to disregard all we had going for us because of one problem. I'd been worrying that I'd chosen wrong, but did I expect that "choosing right" meant never encountering problems and flaws, sometimes big ones? In light of these new insights, that assumption seemed naïve.

In retrospect, I can see how easily I'd believed that "choosing right" would protect me from hard stuff in marriage. This belief had put a lot of pressure on me to make the right choice, which is why I felt so ashamed when I realized that I hadn't done my job well enough. But I had prayed, and I had made the choice to marry my husband in faith. Doubting was tempting, but choosing love and faith was better for my heart, and better for my marriage.

So I continue to choose love, and I will not allow the boogeyman to scare me.

"Forget the former things; **do not dwell on the past.** See, **I am doing a new thing!** Now it springs up; do you not perceive it? I am making a way in the wilderness and streams in the wasteland."

—Isaiah 43:18-19

So often our marriage choices are shaped by our parents' choices. How do those comparisons impact your ability to accept your marriage as it is?

Nicodemus, a respected religious leader, was driven by curiosity to meet Jesus, so he arranged to meet him at night. At that meeting Jesus told him he must be "born again"—a crazy statement on the face of it. But he was telling this follow-the-rules Pharisee that following Jesus would mean a complete transformation of his identity, down to his spiritual DNA. On a scale of 1 to 10 (with 1 representing "no belief" and 10 representing "certainty"), how much do you believe Jesus can truly change a person from the inside out?

Journal the reasons for the number you chose here…

_____

_____

_____

_____

_____

_____

_____

_____

_____

_____

_____

Healing

Here's something only a handful of people knows. When I was 18, I was locked in a room overnight and raped repeatedly.

In a moment, I was changed. No longer innocent. No longer pure. Damaged. Maybe destroyed.

I tried to heal. I tried to put those horrific events behind me. I saw a therapist.

But as the years went by, a pattern emerged. I kept making bad choices. I started doing self-destructive things. I found myself in a series of bad relationships, trying everything I could think of to make them work.

Finally, I had had enough. I realized, deep down, that I was okay on my own. I knew that if marriage was going to be in my future, it would be a gift from

God. If God wanted me to be married, he'd send me a special guy.

And he did.

I fell in love with Dustin.

He was kind, thoughtful, gentle—everything the rapist wasn't.

And yet, in those moments God planned for married couples, those sweet moments of sexual intimacy, all of the memories of my 18-year-old self would wash over me, threatening to drown me.

Screaming, "Stop! Leave me alone! Stop! Stop! Stop!" I would try to push my attacker away. I would feel his foul breath on my face, smell his sweat, see the unrelenting cruelty in his eyes. And once more I would feel the pain of being raped, again and again.

Except this wasn't the stranger who had raped me all those years ago. This was my husband.

My husband, who gently repeated over and over, until I finally heard him: "It's me. It's me. I'm here. I love you. I will never hurt you. It's *me*."

For the first three years of our marriage, I relived the worst night of my life during those times that should have been the most special. And my husband never stopped loving me, never stopped reassuring me, never stopped proving to me that he was the man God intended for me.

We've been married more than 10 years. And Jesus has been in every minute of every day of every one of those years.

Jesus is the great healer. And sometimes he uses marriage to heal us.

"For **I hold you by your right hand**—
I, the Lord your God. And I say
to you, '**Don't be afraid.
I am here to help you.**'"

—Isaiah 41:13, NLT

It's been said that a good marriage helps to heal old wounds while a bad marriage rubs salt into them. Is your marriage more of the healing kind or the salt-rubbing kind? What role have past hurts played in this? How has Jesus used those past hurts as the raw material for forming something beautiful in you? At the end of the day, take a few minutes to journal your thoughts here…

Who Do You Trust?

My husband and I pulled ourselves out of bed early to take a walk, one that ended at my parents' house.

The four of us—Mom, Dad, Barry and I—were chatting in their cozy kitchen as fragrant coffee brewed on the counter. Barry stood and excused himself to head downstairs for a bottle of water.

The rest of us thought nothing about it…until he didn't come back.

I called down the basement steps to see if he was all right, and he asked me to come down and join him.

Here's what I saw: Barry was leaning hard against a wall. He said he was dizzy and his legs felt heavy. And he told me in a shaking voice that he didn't know what was happening to him.

We thought maybe he was overheated from the walk, so we got him onto a couch so he could rest. He closed his eyes and drifted off to sleep.

Several hours later he awoke feeling even worse, and I knew that something was desperately wrong. In the 23 years we'd been married, I'd never seen Barry so sick.

Dad called the paramedics, who arrived with sirens blazing. They gave Barry a once-over and suggested it might be food poisoning, but I knew better. Barry and I had eaten the same dinner, and I felt fine.

One ambulance ride and hospital exam later, a doctor provided a different explanation: vertigo. Something uncomfortable, but Barry could recover at home. The busy ER doc scribbled a signature across discharge papers, but I wouldn't take them.

I didn't know what was spinning my husband's world out of control, but I didn't believe it was anything as simple as vertigo. And I wasn't letting Barry leave the hospital until a better explanation was offered.

Another doctor just coming on shift asked Barry to stand and walk across the room. Something in Barry's gait prompted the physician to order a CT scan, a test that told a different story.

"Your husband has had a massive stroke," a worried doctor told us. The next 24 hours were crucial in determining whether he'd survive.

I was terrified.

How could a healthy, 46-year old man suffer a stroke? And why Barry? He'd always been faithful to Jesus, always lived for him.

And it was there in the hospital consulting room that I heard Jesus speak. He said, "Do you trust me?"

And it was there that I decided, "Yes, I do. Of course I trust you."

The next morning Barry was still with us and looking and feeling better. He'd survived, though it took what felt like endless rounds of physical therapy for him to regain his fine-motor skills and to play the piano again.

And he was home, though he wasn't the same Barry who'd gone downstairs to find a bottle of water. His personality had changed somehow, shifted. With God's help, and the help of family and friends, Barry and I have made it through.

About a month after Barry's stroke, he and I were in a meeting with a brain specialist. She showed us the CT scan ordered by that physician in the hospital and pointed to something at the base of Barry's brain.

"That's the area where the stroke caused damage," she said. "Any swelling—any at all—would have killed him." She leaned back in her chair and shook her head. It was a miracle he'd lived, she said, a miracle he was sitting in the room. She said she couldn't explain it, but we can. My husband, who's playing piano and leading worship in church again, was healed by Jesus.

The Jesus we both trust, no matter what.

"For we **live by faith, not by sight.**"

—2 Corinthians 5:7

As you consider your marriage, how are you walking by faith…and how are you walking by sight? Make a little list below of three or four ways you're actually exercising your faith in the context of your marriage. Ask Jesus for help in surfacing them. Then take a look at your list and be quiet for a moment. Ask Jesus to talk to you about the things on that list. Open yourself to receive whatever he says.

Burdens

"**H**e's been so distant lately," I told my friend one afternoon last year over coffee. "I don't know how to get through to him. He won't let me in. We're drifting apart."

She'd been listening intently, but I could tell she wanted to say something.

"What? What is it?" I pressed.

Biting her lip, she took a deep breath, looked me square in the eyes, and asked, "Are you completely sure he isn't having an affair?"

"He'd never do that," I immediately replied, shaking my head. I'd never seriously considered that his distance signaled unfaithfulness. It couldn't be true.

Over the next few days, her words gnawed at me. In spite of my initial certainty, I began to doubt. I didn't *think* he was seeing someone else, but I'd become increasingly convinced that he was hiding something. Anxious to settle the unease in my heart, I started searching for clues, which eventually led me to our phone records. It was there that I found them: records of calls and texts to a number I didn't recognize. Nervously, I picked up the phone and dialed the number. An unfamiliar woman's voice answered the phone. Shocked, I immediately hung up.

I stood in stunned silence for a couple of minutes, a thousand thoughts and emotions racing through my mind. It wasn't long before one emotion surfaced, stronger than the others: rage.

How *dare* he?

Later that day I confronted him, and he confessed that he'd been talking and texting with this woman for a couple of months. They weren't sleeping together, but it was clear to me that he was already on the road to a full-blown affair. "End the relationship now and go to counseling with me, or this marriage is over," I declared before stomping from the room.

The weeks that followed were some of the hardest in my marriage. It would've been easy to blame my husband for everything that was wrong in our marriage, but I knew I'd played a role, too. What was wrong with me that he felt the need to seek comfort and connection with someone else? How could I not see what had been going on? Most important, how could I fix it?

Every morning I would take a walk, wrestling with these questions again and again. It was a Tuesday when I finally heard Jesus speak words I'll never forget.

"I'll handle this," he said.

With that simple phrase, a huge weight was lifted from my shoulders. I'd been placing all the pressure and responsibility to pull through this on myself. And though not one single question was answered or one problem solved, I suddenly realized that I didn't have to carry the burden of fixing my marriage or the fear of it falling apart. Instead, I could let Jesus carry the burden for me. It was a turning point.

There was still a lot of hard work to come after that Tuesday walk, and still many times when the fear and the hurt and the anger would creep back in. But every time it did, I'd remember that Jesus had offered to take care of it and that my work for the day was to let him.

"**Cast all your anxiety on him**
because he cares for you."

—1 Peter 5:7

Take a minute to think and pray about how much responsibility for your marriage you're placing on your shoulders. What have you been carrying that's so heavy that it's like the straps of a backpack cutting into your shoulders? Instead of carrying that weight, take Jesus up on his offer to carry your burdens for you. Stop right now and offer it to him.

Inviting Jesus

We'd been married for about a year when a friend invited Sarah and me to a Seder, a Jewish Passover meal.

Christians at a Seder miss a *lot* of cultural and religious nuance, but we didn't miss this: opening the door to the prophet Elijah.

As the meal ended, our host family stood up and walked to their front door. They opened it wide, recited psalms together, and then returned to the table.

We followed, wondering at first if we were being invited to leave, but that wasn't what was happening. The Seder tradition is to swing the door open to welcome the prophet and his wisdom to address unanswered questions.

Which, we decided on our drive home, is not a bad tradition.

I forgot about it, but Sarah didn't.

A few weeks later, we were sitting at our kitchen table, the worn red linoleum table papered with bills. We were having what I'd call a discussion, but Sarah clearly saw the conversation differently.

The bills and our budget weren't tallying.

As I was explaining *my* solution to our dilemma, Sarah suddenly shoved back her chair and stood. And then, without a word or backward glance, she stalked out of the kitchen.

I heard the front door open and then…nothing.

She's leaving? I thought. *She's leaving over this?*

Except I never heard the door slammed shut. I found Sarah in the living room, arms crossed, standing in front of the open door.

"What are you doing?" I asked.

Sarah shot me a cool, controlled look. "I'm inviting Jesus in," she said. "We could use a little wisdom right about now."

Ouch.

She was right. We *did* need some wisdom right about then. Then, while the anger was simmering, while the tense silence was driving a wedge between us.

Something between us melted. I took Sarah's hand, and we walked back to the kitchen, where she pulled a third chair up to the table.

"Now that the three of us are here, let's make some decisions," she said.

I'd love to say that she never again had to open the front door, but I'd be lying. That door swung open fairly often at first and then less often as time went on.

But we never did pull that third chair away from the table.

"**If any of you lacks wisdom**, let him **ask God,** who gives generously to all without reproach, **and it will be given him.**"

—James 1:5, ESV

Tense words. A disagreement you've replayed a dozen times. An impasse.

It happens in the best of marriages and the worst…and you'd give anything for a breakthrough.

Learn from this author's example. As a couple, open your front door, walk hand in hand to your kitchen table, and pull out a third chair as you tackle the intractable once more.

Invite wisdom into your conversation. Invite Jesus.

Sex, Rejection, and Risk

I was nervous, and not in a fun, giddy kind of way. My husband and I were about to have sex after what seemed like a really long time, and I was worried that something would go wrong.

"Stop thinking so much!" I chastised myself. "That's not helping! Relax. Try to focus. Quit getting ahead of yourself."

And then for the millionth time I asked God why sex has to be so complicated.

I remember the event that started the dry spell. My husband and I had been making our way to the bedroom when he'd dropped a casual comment about being more playful.

"Why aren't you sexier? I wish you were more like other women who know how to turn on a guy and make sex fun. Can't you try harder?"

Okay, so he didn't *actually* say those words, but that's what I heard beneath his comment about playfulness. "Great," I thought. "So basically you're saying that I'm not enough for you in the bedroom." Well, that killed the mood.

We'd rehashed the conversation a few times since then. I'd told him how rejected I feel when he implies I'm not sexy enough. He'd told me how rejected he feels when I turn him down. And the dry spell continued, my guilt mounting with each passing day. "I should try harder to be more fun," I kept thinking to myself. "I should be like one of those wives who never say no. He wouldn't feel rejected, and maybe sex would get easier."

One night I was reading our kids the story of Peter walking on the water, and the Holy Spirit unexpectedly spoke to me through the story. "Following Jesus means embracing risk," he said. Immediately I thought of our sex life. I wanted it to be safe and risk-free, but the kind of love Jesus invites us to is never risk-free. Jesus himself risked and experienced rejection, including rejection by the people closest to him, his disciples.

No one tells you when you're young and in love that marriage doesn't eliminate rejection. If our sex life was any indicator, my husband and I rejected each other all the time. I'd been feeling ashamed and guilty about this, but the Holy Spirit was showing me through Peter's story, and Jesus' life, that love is supposed to be risky and that rejection is part of the experience.

"Get out of the boat and step onto the water," the Holy Spirit said.

Love is risky—it wouldn't be as powerful if it weren't. I was beginning to wonder if maybe the solution to rejection is not to eliminate all risk but to keep risking and to let Jesus heal us when rejection happens. So I'm getting back into the bedroom. It's not perfect. It's not always fun. But it is risky, and I've learned that's part of love.

"Immediately Jesus made the disciples get into the boat and go on ahead of him to the other side, while he dismissed the crowd. After he had dismissed them, he went up on a mountainside by himself to pray. Later that night, he was there alone, and the boat was already a considerable distance from land, buffeted by the waves because the wind was against it.

"Shortly before dawn **Jesus went out to them, walking on the lake.** When the disciples saw him walking on the lake, they were terrified. **'It's a ghost,' they said, and cried out in fear.**

"But Jesus immediately said to them: **'Take courage! It is I. Don't be afraid.'**

" 'Lord, if it's you,' Peter replied, 'tell me to come to you on the water.'

" 'Come,' he said.

"Then **Peter got down out of the boat, walked on the water and came toward Jesus.** But when he saw the wind, **he was afraid and, beginning to sink,** cried out, 'Lord, save me!'

"Immediately **Jesus reached out his hand and caught him**. 'You of little faith,' he said, **'why did you doubt?'**

"And when they climbed into the boat, the wind died down. Then **those who were in the boat worshiped him, saying, 'Truly you are the Son of God.' "**

—Matthew 14:22-33

Be quiet for a moment and ask Jesus, "What's a little risk I can take on behalf of my marriage right now?" Maybe it's a risk in the bedroom, a risk to open up and trust again, or a risk to try something new. Tomorrow, ask for his input on taking a bigger risk. And the next day, even a bigger one. At the end of the week, consider what impact your risks have made on your relationship, and thank Jesus for the courage and strength to take them.

Spiritual Leadership

The pastor had just finished encouraging all the families in the church to go home and pray together about how to respond to his invitation to serve.

Sitting in the pew a few rows back, I scoffed. *Yeah, right,* I thought. *Like my husband and I are going to do that.* I looked around at the other couples, husbands and wives nodding their heads intently. And then I glanced at the empty space beside me. My husband wasn't even with me that morning; he was at home, watching the game.

I sighed. Who are these couples who pray together over morning devotions? My husband and I barely say good morning to each other as we rush out the door, lukewarm pieces of toast hanging from our mouths. We don't do devotions. We don't hold hands and ask the Lord to guide our day. The idea of trying to get him to do that with me was laughable.

I'd heard plenty of sermons about how the husband is supposed to be the spiritual leader. My husband was spiritual. Sort of. Sometimes. But leader? When it came to spiritual things like church and prayer, I was the one who took the lead. And not very successfully, I might add.

One morning I was praying (okay, complaining) about this lack of husbandly leadership when Jesus stopped me mid-sentence.

"Am I not a good enough leader for you?" he asked. *Awkward.*

"Er…well, of course you are. It's just that he's supposed to be my leader, too, and, well…he's not doing a very good job! I get tired of always being the one bringing you into the equation. Why should I have to do that?"

"Who said you have to keep doing that? Do you think I'm incapable of bringing myself into the equation?" he replied in his nonchalant, Jesus way.

"Uh…"

"Besides," he continued, "what makes you think I'm not leading you *through* your husband? Just because *he* doesn't always make the connection to me doesn't mean it's not there. Can you trust that I'm taking care of your spiritual needs in every way rather than trying to force it to look the way it does for other couples?"

Jesus' argument was persuasive. At the very least it meant I could lay off my husband a bit, which felt kind of…freeing.

So I gave it a try. I backed off. And every time I was irritated by my husband's lack of spiritual leadership, I turned my focus back to Jesus as my spiritual leader, believing he would give me what I needed in his own way.

Did we start having devotions and praying together every morning? Nope. We still don't do those things. But we've had a lot of good spiritual conversations since that time, and since I'm not comparing us to other couples, I've actually noticed them. Backing off has freed me to see my husband's spiritual leadership in new ways and to be grateful for what God's doing uniquely with us.

"Jesus the **author and perfecter of *our* faith**."

—Hebrews 12:2, ASV

Ask Jesus to show you any ways you're trying to micromanage your spouse's spiritual growth. Ask him to give you a key word (maybe "Caution!" or "Whoa!" or "Oops!") to remind you whenever your expectations of your spouse begin to overreach. Invite Jesus to speak that word to you as a guide in your marriage; then change what you're doing when you hear it.

Looking for Nothing in Return

We were watching TV when the doctor called. I could hear my husband's end of the conversation:

"Uh-huh…Yeah, that's right…No, I don't think so… Yes, I understand. You, too. 'Bye."

Anxious, I stared at him, waiting to hear what she'd said.

"It's confirmed. We can't have kids," he replied to my unspoken question.

To say things crumbled after that is an understatement.

Amidst the anger, doubts, and grief, forbidden questions surfaced that no couple wants to ask. Questions like "Did I marry the wrong person? Should we break up and try again with someone else? What if this marriage doesn't work out and it will be too late to start over in time to have kids?"

And then another question: Did I see my husband as a means to motherhood?

During this time, I can say only good things about Jesus. He was gracious and kind and comforting. He saved my faith. He saved me. During this process of saving me, though, he also gently challenged my perspective on marriage. "Marriage is not just a vehicle to fulfill your dream of becoming a mom," he said again and again to me. It was a lesson I needed to learn.

Marriage is not a vehicle to fulfill *any* dream. You don't marry to fulfill the dream of a nice house in a quaint neighborhood. You don't marry to have someone to grow old with. You don't marry to feel loved and admired. Jesus taught me that you marry for love, specifically *his* type of love. *This type of love gives without expecting to receive.*

I'd been expecting my marriage to make me into a mom. I was wrong in this. Jesus' type of love doesn't promise to make dreams come true. But it does promise eternity. For my husband and me, that's a lasting dream, and no diagnosis can take it from us.

"Greater love has no one than this: to lay down one's life for one's friends."

—John 15:13

When you entered into marriage, what are the "things" you expected to get out of it? In the space below, make a quick list of what comes to mind. Don't overthink this. Then, as you scan the list, pause to consider this challenge from Jesus: "Where your treasure is, there your heart will be also." Any spouse would be brokenhearted to learn that he or she is merely a means to an end. And Jesus is brokenhearted over the same dynamic with us. Take a moment to talk to him about your list. Remember the treasure of his presence in your life. Journal your thoughts here…

Spiritual Warfare

He wasn't making any sense. I could tell by the look on his face that he meant every word he was saying, but they were all *so wrong*.

I'd heard his thoughts about his family so many times that I could predict all his talking points, and honestly I was out of ideas. I'd tried playing devil's advocate. I'd tried reasoning with him. I'd tried changing the subject. I'd even tried listening without responding (that one made him really mad, by the way). Nothing had worked. No matter what I did, he was stuck in a loop, and I was being dragged in with him every time the subject came up.

I wanted him to see the truth. I wanted him to open up to grace and forgiveness. I wanted him to be free of these lies and resentments that were tightening around his otherwise good-natured heart. But how could I help him?

Then I heard a friend mention that she'd been experiencing spiritual warfare in her life, including her marriage. "I can feel a difference when I walk through the door at night," she'd said.

Hmm.

Confession: I'm not very "good" at spiritual warfare. Frankly it seems weird to me most of the time. But as I said, I was out of ideas and had nothing to lose. When everything natural isn't working, maybe it's time to look at the supernatural.

I'd heard people pray "spiritual warfare" prayers before. They said things like "Jesus, in your name, I rebuke such and such." This seemed perfectly legitimate...but a little awkward to interject into a conversation with my husband. Phrases like "I plead the blood of Jesus" also seemed like a stretch.

Jesus told me to start in an easier place.

After an argument with my husband, Jesus gave me the idea to write down whatever lies I'd heard spoken. And then, one by one, I prayed for Jesus to dismantle them and replace them with truth. The prayers would be something like this:

"Jesus, this belief of my husband's that his family will never understand him is a lie, and I stand against it. You can bring understanding into any situation. Please deconstruct this lie in his mind and replace it with the truth that he's understood by you, and deeply known by you, and that your understanding is enough. Heal his hurt with your love. Amen."

These prayers haven't changed things overnight, but like my friend, I can tell a difference. Little by little, truth is working its way into our marriage and into our hearts and minds.

"For though we live in the world, we do not wage war as the world does. **The weapons we fight with are not the weapons of the world.** On the contrary, **they have divine power** to demolish strongholds. We demolish arguments and every pretension that sets itself up against the knowledge of God, and we **take captive every thought to make it obedient to Christ."**

—2 Corinthians 10:3-5

Ask the Holy Spirit to bring to light a lie that either you or your spouse has spoken recently, and then take a minute to reflect on the truth. How can you resist the lie and reinforce the truth through prayer and/or action today?

Sacrifice

Nine months into our marriage, my husband suddenly lost his job. I was working for a small-town library on a small-town salary, so we couldn't survive on my income alone, even for as little as a month. While we were trying to figure out what to do, my husband spouted off an idea in passing: "Hey, let's move to Colorado!"

"Yeah, that would be amazing," I dreamily replied, thinking that I was agreeing to a fanciful idea that would fade once reality set in. Little did I know that I was agreeing to an actual plan forming in his head and that he was now applying for jobs exclusively in Colorado.

Surprisingly, he managed to land an interview with a promising company, and, within his first week in Colorado, he was offered the job and found us a place to live.

Once we were both in Colorado, my car broke down, and we couldn't afford to fix it. I couldn't find a job in my field and no longer had the transportation I needed, so I had to work for just above minimum wage at the grocery store across the street until I found a better job. Pretty humbling for a millennial with a Master's degree.

Our two-bedroom apartment cost three times as much as the five-bedroom house we'd been renting in Kansas, and our combined pay was actually less than what we'd been making before we moved, so we struggled constantly with our finances. It took a couple of years to get on our feet again.

I've been asked how I willingly endured all of this, leaving my family, job, and home without completely losing it or even putting up a fight. Well, here's my secret: I'd already given most of that up the day we got married.

Because my husband was in ministry at a different church, I left *my* ministry job so that we could go to church together. I left my cute little apartment that I loved to move into his *very* bachelor house. I spent my savings to help pay off his debts. I sacrificed time with my family and friends to spend time with his.

By the time this move came around, I'd already endured the thousand little deaths that come with the sacrificial plunge into marriage. I knew that in order for this move—and our marriage—to work, we both had to make sacrifices. So that's exactly what we did.

We didn't force each other to make these sacrifices, we didn't keep a running tab of who had sacrificed more, and we didn't allow resentment to take up residence in our hearts (though it certainly tried to several times). We discussed what needed to be done, and we both offered to make our own sacrifices so that we could build a better life together. Our marriage took precedence over our things and our individual comforts.

Underlying it all was the belief that Jesus was guiding us. He was guiding us along a path of love, and this love looked like sacrifice. And this kind of love has equipped us with everything we've needed for our marriage to thrive, regardless of our circumstances.

"For whoever wants to save their life will lose it, but **whoever loses their life for me will save it**"

—Luke 9:24

The love Jesus demonstrated for us is a sacrificial one, and he has planted a similar love in all those who follow him. What are some sacrifices you've made for your marriage that, in truth, you harbor some resentment about? Once something surfaces for you, take a pen and write on the palm of your hand a word that represents that sacrifice. Every time you see that word today, lift your hand a little to give the word to Jesus. Thank him for the opportunity to sacrifice, in love, for your spouse.

Marrying Again

About 300 of us filed into the auditorium, slowly finding seats, most of us avoiding eye contact.

The guest speaker was a seminary professor, a tenured, suited man with several bestsellers under his belt. You might recognize his name if I mentioned it.

He was guest-lecturing on a topic that, I suspect, was the reason most of us had driven across town to hear him: "Is It Permissible for a Christian to Remarry Following Divorce?"

The answer mattered to me.

I didn't choose divorce—at least, not at first. My wife and I had married young, in a hurry, and figured we'd sort it all out as we went. Sure, there were signals that maybe we weren't all that compatible, but didn't love conquer all?

Turns out, it didn't. And on this summer evening, after the house lights dimmed and a glowing introduction of the speaker finally wrapped up, I got my answer.

I couldn't remarry. Not while my former wife was alive. The professor assured us that's what the Bible said and what Jesus endorsed, so that was that.

I understood his theology and Bible references. I'd read them again and again, trying to find a future for myself there. I was 27, alone, and the one person with whom I knew I couldn't make marriage work was—according to the guy on stage—the only woman in the universe available to me.

What I *didn't* understand was how the professor's conclusion could be so unlike the Jesus I knew. The professor spoke in black and white, leaving no room for conversation. He conveyed no empathy while delivering what amounted to a lifetime sentence of solitary confinement.

So I stood up and stayed standing. That's hard to ignore, so, realizing he was losing the crowd, the professor at last pointed to me and asked if I had a question.

I didn't. I had a statement.

"You're speaking for Jesus, but you don't sound like him. I'm not saying you're wrong, but I am saying you're mistaken. You've mistaken the Bible for Jesus."

The professor smiled and raised innocent hands. "I'm only speaking the truth," he said. "It's not popular, but truth seldom is. Jesus was clear, and you'll just have to deal with it. Your problem isn't with me; *your problem is with Jesus.*"

He then resumed his lecture. And I walked out on shaky legs, not looking back.

I paused in the lobby to regain my composure, to think for a moment. *Was* my problem with Jesus? *Was* the issue as clear-cut as the good professor said? I'd confessed my part in the divorce and sensed Jesus calling me to healing, not shame. Had I gotten it all wrong?

The lecture hall door swung open, and a half-dozen people, both men and women, straggled out and over to me. *Great*, I thought, *bouncers.*

They stood there, shuffling awkwardly, until one of the men finally said, "Okay, I for one can't accept what he said without hating Jesus."

And that was it in a nutshell. Here we were, a wounded group of Jesus-followers, wondering if we could be forgiven. Wondering if Jesus might give us a reset. Wondering if we could pull the scarlet D's off our foreheads and move on with life.

We'd heard "no" from the professor...but might Jesus give us hope?

Well, I remarried. We're 33 years in at last count, and I'm confident we'll go the distance. If marrying my second—and last—wife was a sin, it's one Jesus has forgiven, and he's standing with us. I know that's true because I asked him to be with us and, when I hear his voice, it's spoken not from a distant stage but from close beside me.

Jesus made my marriage possible by pouring out forgiveness and hope. He keeps my marriage possible by continuing to do so.

How has Jesus shown he's committed to my marriage? By showing up.

Every. Single. Day.

"Look! I stand at the door and knock. If you hear my voice and **open the door, I will come in, and we will share a meal together as friends.**"

—Revelation 3:20, NLT

Is there a difference between following the Bible and following Jesus? Why or why not? Is Jesus fundamentally hard or fundamentally soft? Explain.

Expecting Jesus to simply rubber-stamp everything we do with forgiveness is called "cheap grace." How do you deal with the tension of your brokenness, its consequences, and Jesus' offer to forgive? Write your response here...

Walking Away From Faith

Things began falling apart, ironically enough, on Easter. My family and I were traveling abroad a few years ago, visiting exotic locations we had dreamed about our entire lives. But as much fun as we were having, there was something unsettling lurking in the shadows of my marriage.

The next-to-last day of our trip happened to land on Easter Sunday. We hid chocolate eggs around the hotel room for our youngest son to find. But when our teenage daughter wondered aloud, "Are we going to celebrate the real Easter?" I had to admit I had no plans.

Later that night, Shannon, my wife, asked, "What's going on? You used to be the spiritual leader of our family, but now…"

This was the moment I'd been dreading for a couple of years. The moment I knew I had to be completely honest with the woman I'd been married to for 20 years.

"I'm not sure what I think anymore," I admitted. "I've had some serious doubts for a couple of years, and I'm not sure I believe in God."

It was a kick in the gut for Shannon, to say the least.

She was hurt, and I couldn't blame her. From her perspective, I wasn't the same man she'd married. She'd made a lifelong commitment to a guy who was faithful to God. I'd gone to church since birth, attended Christian schools and college, and even served in various leadership positions in the church. I knew the Bible inside and out. My constant faith had been an anchor in our relationship. But now, as far as Shannon could tell, that anchor was lost at sea.

On a deeper level, she was hurt because I hadn't been honest with her about my doubts. She'd been experiencing a crisis of faith herself and had told me about it on a couple of occasions. Yet I hadn't been open with her about my own struggles. I'd kept it a secret. (And when it comes to marriage, secrets are bad.)

Although I'd never been unfaithful, she felt betrayed.

Things went downhill from there. Shannon lost all trust in me. She said she didn't know who I was anymore. Fighting became a habit. We'd go whole weeks without talking to each other. For the first time, we disagreed about how to raise our kids. We slept in different rooms. We even hated each other, off and on. The bad days far outnumbered the good ones. About a miserable year and a half later we decided to divorce. We agreed to have dinner the next evening to talk about the details.

Twenty years isn't an easy thing to throw away. Neither is your faith.

Shannon and I talked over fajitas. (Is that a weird detail to remember?) We realized that beneath the brokenness and pain, we still loved each other. But if we were going to make our relationship work, things had to be different somehow. So we each made a promise to do one thing to keep our marriage alive. My promise was to try to rediscover my faith.

I won't pretend it was easy. For most of my life, my belief in Jesus had been automatic. It was something I'd been born into, and I took it for granted. I knew I had to relearn Jesus. I connected with like-minded bloggers and authors who'd walked the same spiritual path. I had a couple of close friends who helped me talk things out. I reread the Bible from different perspectives. Most significantly, Shannon and I talked openly about our hard questions and the difficult things in the Bible. *A lot.*

And I was surprised to find a new kind of Jesus.

Jesus was no longer the fabled storybook character of my childhood. (Or, to be honest, the fabled storybook character of my adulthood.) This new Jesus was someone who stood for the things I needed most in my life—grace, compassion, forgiveness—that Shannon and I were more likely to get from each other than anywhere else.

Rather than merely studying Jesus or talking about Jesus or thinking about Jesus, I'm learning what it really means to *abide* in Jesus.

Here's the amazing part: The new things I learned about Jesus applied to my relationship with Shannon, too. We've become Jesus to each other. We love, share, trust, give, shine, and seek. All the things Jesus called us to do, we try to live out in our lives together.

Sure, I've adjusted some of my theological views. I read the Bible differently now. I don't have to be right, or 100 percent certain, or perfect, or doubtless. I just have to *be*. And I can honestly say that Jesus means more to me now than he ever has. His truth is more real than it's ever been.

Shannon told me the other day she thinks I'm much more Christian now than I was before my season of disbelief. That means a lot to me, and it's a sign of how far we've come.

"As the Father has loved me, so have I loved you. **Abide in my love.**"

—John 15:9, ESV

Consider the ways you and your spouse have changed since your wedding (including improvements!) and how you've both grown as a result. Today, start a simple new habit that will deepen your appreciation for Jesus and your attachment to him. Every day read a few verses (or more, if you want) from one of the four Gospels—Matthew, Mark, Luke, or John. As you read, ask yourself a simple question again and again: "What's one thing I know for sure about Jesus, based only on what I just read?" After you've been experimenting with this for a month, ask yourself how your relationship with Jesus—and with your spouse—has changed. Write what you observe below and on the following page.

...

Surveillance

I was cleaning the house on a Saturday morning when I found the first clue—the clue that my husband was making bad choices and hiding them from me.

The incident wasn't a deal-breaker, and I thought maybe it would be the last. It wasn't. Along came another and another, and with them came the gnawing realization that there would be more.

I couldn't escape the feeling that I wasn't getting the full story, and I wasn't sure what to do. Every day that passed with me still in the dark was another day for my inner voice to tell me I was being codependent or naïve or in denial. Every new day was a day that he could be taking advantage of me.

I really wanted to get to the truth, so I started considering ways I could discover all of my husband's secrets. I thought about installing a tracking device to find out if he really was working late. I considered installing hidden cameras in the house to see what he was up to when I wasn't home. I contemplated getting home early from work, surprising him, or calling his work every few hours to catch him off guard. I wondered about following him when he left the house.

Then something unexpected happened: God told me to do nothing. No spying. No surveillance. Instead, he encouraged me to pray for the truth to come out on its own. So every night I prayed for peace and protection and the strength to handle the truth when it finally emerged. And then I went to sleep.

One morning at 4:00, I sensed God shake me awake. "Get up. The truth is in his workshop, in the file cabinet." And there it was: a flood that would start a storm in our marriage. Those were some of the hardest days of my life, but God protected me, gave me the strength I needed, and filled me with peace.

I know that hiring a private detective or using the latest surveillance technology would have uncovered the truth a lot earlier. But that would have made revealing the truth *my* job, and I didn't want that burden. I discovered the freedom of allowing Jesus to carry it. He promises to shine light into darkness. And once the dark things were no longer hidden, it was that light that continued to guide me.

"There is nothing hidden that will not be disclosed, and nothing concealed that will not be known or brought out into the open."

—Luke 8:17

Jesus says he is the truth and brings whatever is secret into the light. Think about something that needs to be brought to light in your marriage, and ask Jesus to reveal that truth. Then resist the urge to "help him along" by trusting Jesus' timing and methods.

What About Sex?

Is it still a marriage when the sex stops?

That's a question that's never felt safe to ask aloud, especially at church. And, truth be told, it's never felt safe to ask anywhere else.

Unsafe because asking it is embarrassing. Unsafe because the last thing I need is free advice from people who don't understand or, even worse, people who think they understand but don't.

So for the past decade I've kept the question—and the problem—to myself.

It's not worth bringing up with my wife again. Counseling hasn't helped. And prayer? In spite of all the happy Christian promises that "prayer changes things," it hasn't changed that.

So why keep raising the topic…with her or with Jesus? Neither seems to care.

Marriage is for better and worse, sicker and poorer, but what about one partner just losing interest in sex? Not because of abuse, illness, or anything else she can or will explain, but just because?

Then what?

Several years into unwanted abstinence, I gave up, too. Gave up asking. Gave up reaching over to caress her. Stony silence is a powerful incentive to cease and desist…so I did just that.

Yet I couldn't give up circling back to the question: Is it still marriage when the sex stops? It's a friendship, sure, and a partnership. But is it marriage?

Here's what doesn't help answer that question: Bible study. Sermons. Marriage encounter weekends where it's a winking assumption that couples will show up late for morning sessions because they've had marathon encounters in bed.

What helped answer the question—for me, anyway—was a question I swear I heard spoken aloud even though that wasn't possible.

Early one morning on my commute to work, I was thinking about my situation. Not praying, exactly, but just holding the dilemma in my mind. Should I stay in the marriage, cut my losses and leave it—what was the best move? I was standing at a crossroads, looking at different paths snaking out in different directions. Which should I take?

That's when I heard it: "How's *our* marriage?"

Male voice, not mine. In the car. While I was alone and doing 70 on I-5. I nearly swerved off the road.

Was it Jesus speaking? To this day I'm not sure, but I think so because he asked a question that pulled me out of self-pity into a new place.

As a Christian, I'm the bride of Christ. And to be honest, I've never been especially interested in intimacy with him. I know it's a very pale comparison, but what I was missing in my marriage was physical intimacy and what Jesus was missing from me was emotional intimacy.

They're not the same, I know that. But they're not all that different, either.

Maybe, if I was being distant in my marriage with Jesus, I was being distant in my marriage with my wife, too. Maybe our absentee sex life wasn't all her fault after all.

I'd love to tell you everything is fixed now, but it isn't. After so long maybe it takes an equal amount of time for what's frozen to thaw, for what's broken to be mended.

But here's what's different: I'm all in, heart and soul. It's not just commitment that's keeping me in my marriage; it's love.

And I have to believe love can do what disappointment can't.

"Wives, submit yourselves to your own husbands as you do to the Lord... Husbands, love your wives, just as Christ loved the church and gave himself up for her."

—Ephesians 5:22, 25

These verses are often trotted out as a formula or, worse yet, as weapons to flog uncooperative spouses. But what if you heard them less as "shoulds" and more as insights Jesus shares through Scripture that set you up for healing and greater marital success? What if you received them…gratefully?

Journal your response to that suggestion, and then ask Jesus, "What do you think about what I wrote?"

_____

_____

_____

_____

_____

_____

_____

When Tragedy Strikes

There wasn't even time to gasp a prayer.

One moment we were sailing down a country road toward a family Thanksgiving dinner at my sister-in-law's house. The next, the sudden swerve of an SUV into our lane changed our lives forever.

I regained consciousness slowly, pinned behind the steering wheel. Beside me was Bill, my wife's brother, who'd been catapulted over the passenger seat and slammed against the dashboard.

Beneath Bill lay Frances, my mother-in-law…dead.

And somewhere crushed in the back seat was Mary, my wife.

Mary—who wasn't moving. Or speaking. Or, as far as I could tell, even breathing.

Mary survived the crash, barely. So did I, as did Bill. Crushed bones, fractured legs and shoulders, collapsed lungs, concussions—a long list of injuries required one surgery after another and therapies that stretched on for a year...and stretch on still.

And then there was the shattered, lifeless body of Frances, crumpled in the twisted metal.

Tragedies often tear marriages apart, and one reason may be this: Along with tragedies come questions, some of which can't be answered.

Why did this happen? Why us? And how can we trust a Jesus who *could have* nudged us past the point of impact without a scratch?

Mary and I know not to chase after unanswerable questions because we've been here before.

Fracturing a leg in a motorcycle accident torpedoed my appointment to the Naval Academy. Shortly after Mary and I were married, she was diagnosed with a brain tumor. We've weathered a dozen health and financial disasters. Survived layoffs, kid crises, and relational storms.

So again and again this past year, we've intentionally recalled how Jesus has been faithful through all those tragedies. How he's proven himself a steady rock on which to build our lives and marriage. How he might not fix what's broken in our lives, but he's walked through all the brokenness with us.

Have I gotten angry with him? Yes—but he's big enough to handle my anger.

"Understand, therefore, that the Lord your God is indeed God. He is the faithful God who keeps his covenant for a thousand generations and **lavishes his unfailing love on those who love him and obey his commands.**"

—Deuteronomy 7:9, NLT

How have the tragedies you've faced impacted your marriage? In what ways have they drawn you and your spouse closer together or driven a wedge between you?

How has Jesus been faithful to you and your marriage? List ways you've seen that. Then prayerfully read aloud what you've written, letting the words sink deeply into your heart and soothe your soul.

Jesus Broke Into My Marriage

When I was very young, about 5 years old, I began to believe a lie. The lie was small and innocent but began to grow during my teenage years. The falsehood was born out of a mixture of the teaching of my church and the shaping influence of my parents, and it went something like this: *You aren't good enough. You don't try hard enough to be good. You're a disappointment. God is not pleased with you. Try harder!* It wasn't until my life and marriage unraveled in my 40s that I was able to face and name the lie: Its name is *shame*.

Growing up was a mostly happy immersion in family and church. I was rewarded for doing the "right" things, especially at church. I didn't dare step out of bounds and do "wrong" things, even though I often thought that would be more fun. I lived a life of compliance and performance, while hiding any flaws in my character or missteps in my behavior. It was my job to make my parents and my pastor proud, without much awareness of Jesus. I felt I could never do enough to please him, so I marginalized him. I found ways to keep him at bay, not letting him have his way with me. I didn't understand how to give or receive love, especially within the religious world in which I was immersed.

That pervasive voice of shame never stopped whispering lies to me. In fact, it grew more persistent and harder to ignore *after* I married my wife. Almost every conversation with her brought a deeper emotional reaction because my shame altered her words into expressions of condemnation. As I had done with Jesus, I felt I could never do enough to please her, so I marginalized her. I found ways to keep her at bay—by being busy in my work, by being angry at insignificant things, by twisting her words to confirm my shame.

Ironically, I sought escape from my shame and religious performance by having an affair. Since I believed I was a disappointment, I determined to become one. The affair was a horrible choice, and the consequences were horrific. I hurt so many people: my children, my sisters, my friends, the person with whom I chose to have the affair.

Most tragically, I crushed my wife with that selfish and self-loathing choice.

I was a fool who was desperate to escape my mess by any possible means. I didn't believe that anything or anyone could rescue my marriage, repair the damage I'd done to my wife, or bring the lies of shame into the light.

Then Jesus broke into my darkness in the most astonishing and unexpected way.

When I confessed the affair to my wife, I expected to be tossed from her life. Her reaction was terrifying; she literally writhed in pain. I've no doubt that she wanted to be rid of me at first, she was so badly hurt.

Instead, she invited Jesus into her pain. Over the span of several agonizing months, she stopped fighting my patterns of anger and meanness, responding to me with uncontrived kindness instead. She moved toward me rather than condemning me or pushing me away. She stopped reacting to my volatility. She honestly showed me her hurt, and her authentic expression of sorrow over my betrayal jolted me. Then, very slowly, she forgave me. She didn't just say the words "I forgive you"; she demonstrated that forgiveness freely and generously. Tenderly.

I don't know exactly when it happened, but I began to see Jesus. Real, personal, gritty truth about my sin and all. I understood and knew her pain, and I began to see his pain. Her determination to trust Jesus in her suffering showed me how he trusted his Father as he suffered and paid the price for all sin on the cross. She was genuine and called me to be real, too. She embraced me and loved me despite my mess. She showed me grace, mercy, and faith. She showed me who Jesus is.

We're both still healing, and I continue to be haunted by the shadows of shame, both real and imagined. Our path to health hasn't been simple or easy; rather, it's often hard and bumpy. But Jesus has been present and active in each stumbling step.

Ultimately, I didn't get what I deserved. I didn't get what I expected. I got introduced to the real Jesus by my wife. I love her for that gift and so much more. He is my only hope for healing. He is my only hope for love. She is my best friend and partner.

We're growing old together, learning new rhythms of grace in our lives. Our love is much more genuine. We're somehow able to look past each other's flaws (at least most of the time!). We share a love that's both inspired by and empowered by Jesus. It is he who taught this broken and shame-infused man what it means to be loved and forgiven, transformed by mercy and grace. All through the heart of my wife.

"For God, who said, 'Let there be light in the darkness,' has **made this light shine in our hearts so we could know the glory of God** that is seen in the face of Jesus Christ."

—2 Corinthians 4:6, NLT

Ask Jesus to reveal the lies you've believed about yourself. Wait in silence and write whatever comes to you. Then ask him how those lies have been affecting your relationship with your spouse. Again, wait in silence and write whatever comes to you. Now ask him a simple question: "What must I do to be healed?"

Empty

I wasn't aware that our marriage was dissolving until it was nearly over.

We'd had our ups and downs over the course of 20 years, but I was generally content. My husband, Mark, loved his career, and I loved mine. Our son was successfully launched. We had lots of true-blue friends. We had a close and loving extended family. We were devoted to our house, garden, and dogs. If anyone had asked me about my life, I would have said, "I have a great life."

Of course, there were reasons to stress out. The great recession had reduced my husband's earnings to a tenth of what they had been. At the same time, my job had gotten much bigger—more exciting, to be sure, but much more consuming than it had ever been.

Over the years, our circle of friends had broadened, and I found myself spending more and more time with this group or that, going on weekend trips with girlfriends, planning book club meetings, gathering each week with a prayer group. Most of my family had moved into our area in the last several years, and I was thrilled to be able to spend more time with them as well. Weekends were spent cleaning the house, doing the laundry, mowing, weeding, having friends over…You know the drill.

And then our marriage started to fracture. Mark had developed a snoring habit that made sleeping together impossible, so we slept in separate rooms. Much of the physical closeness I'd cherished, waking up next to him every morning and falling asleep by his side every night, was gone. He would get home from business trips grumpy and distant. He seemed to be drinking more, and when he drank he was unpredictable and obnoxious. We drifted further and further apart until we seemed like nodding acquaintances rather than husband and wife. Distance turned to misery the day he refused to help me with a chore that I wasn't physically able to do by myself, saying, "I don't care. Do it yourself."

Then one day I discovered some emails on his computer and a pattern of text messages on our phone bill that made it clear he was having an affair.

I was no longer the woman Mark loved. I was shattered.

And I was reminded of how much I loved him.

We agreed to see a counselor, and we plowed through some really painful issues. For at least two years, it was a one-step-forward, two-steps-back process. But finally I began to experience more hope than despair and really felt we were making solid progress.

Until the night he was away on another business trip and I found more text messages.

I was done. I planned the conversation we would have when he got home. I would tell him I wanted a divorce. We would somehow have to figure out how to divide up the life we had shared into two equal parts. I was convinced that this was the only way forward.

The day he was to return was a Sunday. That morning I went to church with my sister and nephew and sat through the service, miserably contemplating the conversation I was planning to have that afternoon. When we emerged from church and were walking to our cars, my sister said, "Well, I guess you got your answer."

"About what?" I asked.

"About Mark. It was pretty clear."

"It was? What answer did you hear?"

"That you should stick with him, of course. Didn't you get that?"

Stunned, I said, "No. I didn't hear anything."

My nephew chimed in. "Wow. I thought it was about as clear as it could get."

I sat in my car, truly in a state of shock. I was at a complete loss. I cried out to God, "I don't know what to think. I don't know what to feel. I have no answers. Nothing I've tried has worked. And now you've apparently vetoed the only solution that makes sense. God, help me. Do whatever you want with me. Use me however you want. I'm empty."

And I meant it. For the first time in my life, I yearned for God to take complete charge of everything—my thoughts, my emotions, my actions, my reactions, everything.

I got home and waited for Mark to return from his trip. I had no plan. No carefully rehearsed speech. No ideas. I had nothing.

When he walked in the door, we greeted each other warily. Then I said, "How was your trip?"

He sat down in a chair a few feet from mine and started telling me about it. He'd been gone two weeks and had met all kinds of interesting people and had some great experiences. As I sat there, simply listening, a silent question formed in my mind: "When was the last time you were fully present to your husband?"

That was the turning point in our marriage.

Something miraculous happened during that two-hour conversation. My husband would probably say that was when he finally sensed that I really did love him.

I would say that was when I allowed Jesus to be the Lord of my life.

"Whoever finds their life will lose it,
and **whoever loses their life for
my sake will find it.**"

—Matthew 10:39

The Bible is full of seeming paradoxes like this, paradoxes that turn our understanding of life, ourselves, and our marriages upside down. How has your marriage illustrated this? Take some time to write your response here…

Sustainer

It was the turkey dinner that did it. That's when we knew.

Starting out in marriage is always challenging, but when you're a young couple serving in ministry at a small church, you have a few extra issues.

One of those was the old house trailer the church purchased to be our home. Yes, we were grateful...but not all the time.

Like when the furnace would stop running for no apparent reason.

On those occasions, the trailer got so cold that not only would the water in the toilet freeze but so would the water in the goldfish bowl. (By the way, I'm here to report that goldfish *can* recover from being mini frozen goldfish sticks.)

And there was a refrigerator that worked well but came with a mysterious hot pad hanging on the front. When I looked behind the pad, I found a hole through which a rifle slug had passed.

I pried the slug out of the refrigerator's insulation and rehung the hot pad. Some questions aren't worth asking.

We tried viewing our trailer as a sign of Jesus' provision, of his faithfulness to a fresh young couple doing their best to hear his will for their lives.

But when you wake up to a bathroom that won't work and a frozen fish, that can rattle your confidence.

The fast-food job I took to help us make ends meet came with a promise of a quick promotion to a better-paying management position, but that didn't happen.

For the first time in our relationship, we didn't laugh much. I had trouble looking her in the eye, ashamed that I wasn't providing for her.

And with just days between us and our car being repossessed, we found ourselves wondering: Had we gotten this right?

Does Jesus really take care of those who seek him?

Did he even know we were there?

Had he forgotten us?

And then the turkey dinner showed up at our door.

Our church shared a building with a small Christian school, and many of the school parents knew our situation. So, following a school dinner, they hiked over to our trailer and brought with them a reminder that we weren't alone.

A turkey, with all the trimmings. Crates of canned goods. Enough food to fill our empty shelves and bring tears to our eyes.

The promised promotion arrived in short order, and so did the dollars we needed to hold on to our car—and our ministry.

And this young couple discovered a truth that has sustained us through 42 years of marriage: Jesus never forgets his people. He walks with us through the most difficult, impossible times.

"For I know the plans I have for you, declares the Lord, **plans for welfare and not for evil, to give you a future and a hope.** Then you will call upon me and come and pray to me, and I will hear you. You will seek me and find me, when you seek me with all your heart."

—Jeremiah 29:11-13, ESV

The same God who spoke those words to his people thousands of years ago came to your wedding. Why do you think he'd desert you when there's difficulty in your marriage?

Pause. Take a deep breath. And as you exhale, let your sigh be a sign of praise. As an act of faith, simply say out loud, "Jesus, I believe you are with me, and I believe you are 'working everything for good' in my marriage."

Awe

Clutching my husband's arm, I snuggled close and buried my nose in the warmth of his shoulder.

A chill filled the night air as the boat motored back to the dock. Even though we were still drying off after our ocean dip, my love for Thom warmed me. We exchanged no words and just held each other close.

We had just shared an experience that only God could orchestrate.

We'd joined a nighttime snorkeling adventure in Hawaii. On our way to the site, dolphins and humpback whales wowed us by swimming beside our boat. The captain marveled that we'd witnessed such a special treat. I agreed.

Once we arrived at the dive site, we donned our snorkel gear, lowered ourselves into the ocean, and grabbed hold of a rectangular apparatus with lights in the middle, all designed to attract manta rays.

Thom and I and a dozen others expectantly clung to the floating rectangle. Our guide instructed us to stay still. No kicking. (I loved that, since MS has robbed my legs of most of their strength and responsiveness.)

We floated there, waiting. Watching through our masks, breathing through our snorkels, peering into the ocean depths.

Then...

From below arose a manta ray. Like an alien spaceship, this giant glided beneath us. And then it swam beside us, coming close, touching us. Silky, sleek, smooth.

My husband and I watched, shoulder to shoulder, as nature unfurled itself beneath and around us. One manta ray. Then another. Then another. Their black tops somersaulted to reveal their white undersides, vents, and wide mouths. I squealed with delight through my snorkel.

Watching God's creation showing off like this—and getting to share it with my best friend/husband— deeply touched my soul.

I silently thanked Jesus for giving us the gift of this shared experience.

Then I realized we didn't have to be on a special dive in Hawaii to share this bond.

Nature brings us together wherever we are. We marvel at small miracles like the hummingbird that frequents our deck. We celebrate sunsets. Thom rolls his eyes when the farm girl in me relishes the smell of fresh rain when it first splashes against dry earth. We bask in the golden hour at dusk. Every day God lavishes us with gifts from his creation.

My heart is full of gratitude for those gifts. And sharing them with my husband somehow expands and multiplies them.

"In the beginning God created the heavens and the earth...And God saw that it was good...Then the Lord God said, **'It is not good for the man to be alone. I will make a helper who is just right for him.'** "

—Genesis 1:1, 12; 2:18, NLT

Look around you. Jot down miracles of nature, large and small. Then ask Jesus how each might be a metaphor for your marriage. Ask him to reveal what you love most about your spouse. Write that, too. Then thank Jesus for all that is good in your life and in your marriage.

Boundaries

I was living life, making the best of what it threw at me, and suddenly it was as if I had shaken myself awake only to realize this wasn't the life I expected. Not the life I wanted.

My wake-up moment came when I realized my husband was using methamphetamines. And not just using—he was an addict. After traveling a long, tortuous road, Jason eventually overcame his addiction to meth. But he continued to hide in a haze of marijuana.

I cried. I coped. I turned to Jesus, whose love became the sanctuary my marriage couldn't provide. Jesus, whose love encouraged me to do what I'd been unwilling to do for nearly a decade.

I drew a healthy boundary. The drugs would have to go, or my husband would.

This is where, on the Lifetime channel, Jason would realize the enormity of the loss he was facing, tearfully repent, and change everything.

Not so much.

Faced at last with a boundary, Jason silently packed a duffel bag and moved out into a bachelor life he found more satisfying than our marriage. I was devastated...but not alone. Jesus stood with me.

Our story hasn't ended in divorce. Jason and I are together again, but only after months of painful separation.

And here's the good news, at least to me: *Jason returned to a marriage I can live with*. Our marriage now makes room for Jesus. And it doesn't accommodate Jason's marijuana mistress.

Setting boundaries is seldom easy. But, as Jesus made clear to me, it can be the right thing to do. It was certainly the right thing to do in our situation.

Jesus himself drew plenty of boundaries. I just didn't know he would one day give me permission—and the courage—to draw a boundary of my own.

"My brothers and sisters, **if one of you should wander from the truth** and someone should bring that person back, remember this: **Whoever turns a sinner from the error of their way will save them from death** and cover over a multitude of sins."

—James 5:19-20

Demonstrating unconditional love within the confines of healthy boundaries can be tricky. Have you ever had to draw a healthy boundary in your marriage? In retrospect, what would you do differently? What role did Jesus play in the process? Journal your thoughts in the space below.

Angry at God

On August 6, 2015, my friend Amy passed a life insurance physical with flying colors. The life insurance company rated Amy's health in the very top tier, so they gave her their lowest possible rate for her new insurance policy.

Six days later, she was diagnosed with Stage IV-B peritoneal cancer and was scheduled for extensive surgery on August 19.

She endured months of extended treatments with six different forms of chemotherapy. She was unable to eat solid food for nearly a year. She faced one painful setback after another, as each new treatment or option or idea would give her hope, only to be told two weeks later, "Well, that's not working, so…"

She spent long days and nights in the hospital and lost her beautiful long brown hair and much of her body weight.

But she never stopped loving. She loved Jesus, her husband, her family, and her friends with a wholehearted purity that left us breathless.

She spent her last weeks writing letters to all of her family members. And she wrote 18 years of future birthday cards to her young grandchildren, as well as future wedding and graduation cards.

Amy died on September 11, 2016.

Throughout her illness, her husband, Mike, used a private Facebook page to keep their large circle of friends updated.

The day Amy entered hospice, Mike posted this:

Somebody asked me recently why I'm not angry at God.

I had to think about that for a moment because, honestly, it never occurred to me to be angry at him. I understand that this is an awful situation. Not only is my wife dying, but she is suffering. And all I can do is stand helplessly by while the suffering takes its toll, knowing (as we all do) where this road ends. What I don't understand is why that should make me angry at God.

In the first place, anger toward God is beyond futile. My anger changes nothing about him, me, or my circumstances. Why bother with self-destructive behavior if it doesn't bring hope or healing or even some measure of relief? That just seems stupid.

But really, the answer to the original question is another question: Why would I lash out in anger toward the only thing that brings me solace? That'd be akin to punching the lifeguard who's trying to save me from drowning.

In this awful situation, I'm not warmed by anger or comforted by bitterness. It's only Christ's Holy Spirit who brings me peace, who walks beside me in sorrow, who gives me hope not just for tomorrow, but also for today, for the next hour, for the next 10 minutes. It's Christ's constant presence that gives Amy and me moments of unexpected joy, of laughter, of kinship, of determination. Why would I ever push that away in exchange for a futile blame game toward the One who carries and comforts when I feel like I can't walk another step or stop crying long enough to see the sunshine? I must cling to Christ, desperately, determinedly, gratefully, for strength to see myself through every moment, both good and hurtful, both joyful and sorrowful. And so that's what I do. I've found Jesus to be more than sufficient. He is a man of sorrows who knows how to share mine, and who tells me gently, in ways that I can believe, that in the end, everything is going to be okay. God is good; he is always good.

"The Lord is good, a strong refuge when trouble comes. He is close to those who trust in him"

—Nahum 1:7, NLT

What do you believe, in the deepest part of your soul, about God? Do you believe, as Mike does, that Jesus is truly, always, thoroughly good? What evidence in your life do you have for this, and what evidence has challenged it?

Spend some time in prayer, asking God to show you who he is and who you are in light of that.

Your Story

When we started this project, we thought a few people would be willing to tell us about the challenges and joys they've experienced in their marriages. We were astounded when *every single one* of the people we asked opened their hearts to us. They spoke of pain, healing, grace, and Jesus. Again and again, they described how Jesus had intervened in their hearts and in their marriages, transforming both.

And they all talked about how freeing it was to tell their stories. It was liberating for them to realize they're not the only ones who've faced rough patches in their marriages. It was cathartic to describe those times. And it was beautiful to recall God's faithfulness, to remember how he had lifted them up and set their feet on higher ground, again and again. They all thanked us for encouraging them to remember.

So we'd like to do the same for you.

We'd like the last story in this book to be yours.

Write your story here…or type it and then tape it here.

And as time passes and your marriage evolves, continue to add to your story.

It's a story well worth remembering and retelling.

"We will use these stones to build a memorial. In the future your children will ask you, 'What do these stones mean?' Then you can tell them, 'They remind us that the Jordan River stopped flowing when the Ark of the Lord's Covenant went across.' **These stones will stand as a memorial among the people of Israel forever."**

—Joshua 4:6-7, NLT

Where will Jesus interrupt you?

Dreaded chore...or a chance to slow down and pay attention to Jesus? When we invite Jesus to interrupt every moment of our lives—not just the quiet, tidy ones— suddenly even chores take on a whole new purpose.

For books, Bibles, devotions, planners, and coloring experiences that move Jesus into EVERY corner of your life, visit...

JesusCenteredLife.com

#JesusInterruption

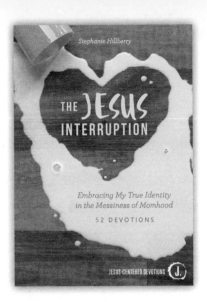

52 Faith-Building Devotions for Moms Who Live in the Real World

You'd light a scented candle and ponder the Bible cover-to-cover if you had time...but that's not going to happen.

Fortunately, Jesus stands ready to connect with you—even in the messiness of mom-hood. *Especially* in the messiness.

These 52 do-them-whenever devotions will help you see, hear, and embrace Jesus. They're Jesus interruptions—moments in the mess you can reach out to Jesus and feel the warmth of him reaching back to you.

Find *The Jesus-Interruption* and other Jesus-centered resources at JesusCenteredLife.com.